Through a Night of Horrors

Through a Night of Horrors

Voices from the 1900 Galveston Storm

EDITED BY

Casey Edward Greene

&

Shelly Henley Kelly

TEXAS A&M UNIVERSITY PRESS
COLLEGE STATION

Copyright © 2000 by Rosenberg Library
Manufactured in
the United States of America
All rights reserved
Second edition, 2002

All photos courtesy Rosenberg Library, Galveston, Texas

frontispiece: "Victims of the Galveston Flood,"
sculpted by Pompeo Coppini, San Antonio, 1904

*Publication of this volume
is made possible by a generous grant
from the Rosenberg Library, Galveston, Texas.*

The paper used in this book
meets the minimum requirements
of the American National Standard
for Permanence of Paper
for Printed Library Materials, z39.48-1984.
Binding materials have been chosen for durability.

Library of Congress Cataloging-in-Publicaton Data

Through a night of horrors : voices from the 1900
Galveston storm / edited by Casey Edward Greene
and Shelly Henley Kelly.

p. cm.

Includes bibliographical references and index.

ISBN 0-89096-961-2 (cloth);

1-58544-228-3 (pbk.)

1. Galveston (Tex.)—History—20th
century—Sources. 2. Hurricanes—Texas—
Galveston—History—20th century—Sources.
3. Floods—Texas—Galveston—History—20th
century—Sources. 4. Galveston (Tex.)—
Biography. 5. Oral history. I. Greene, Casey
Edward, 1954– II. Kelly, Shelly Henley, 1971–

F394.G2 T49 2000

976.4'139—dc21 00-029886

Dedicated to the survivors
who rebuilt Galveston for our future.

"I am here and my fingers are in the wound,
and I assure you that the side was pierced
and the nails did go through."
—CLARA BARTON

CONTENTS

Preface IX
Introduction 3

Survivor Letters

Anonymous 13
John D. Blagden 15
George Hodson 19
Charles W. Law 23
Sarah D. Hawley 28
Winifred Black 36
Martin Nicholson 42
Walker W. Davis 45
Alice Block 49
Eleanor Hertford 52
Joseph Henry Hawley 56
James Brown 63
Winnifred Clamp 66
Ida Smith Austin 67

Survivor Memoirs

Lloyd R. D. Fayling 75
Ben C. Stuart 94
Thomas L. Monagan 101
Gordon Gaither 104

Louisa Hansen Rollfing 106
Arnold R. Wolfram 118
Henry Cortes 124
Harry I. Maxson 129
Geneva Dibrell Scholes 139

Survivor Oral Histories

Emma Beal 149
Henry Bettencourt 151
Margaret Rowan Bettencourt 152
Hyman Block 155
William Mason Bristol 161
R. Wilbur Goodman 164
John W. Harris 168
Mary Louise Bristol Hopkins 170
Ellen Edwards Nilson 174
Katherine Vedder Pauls 179

Notes 187
Bibliography 199
Index 203

PREFACE

The September 8, 1900, hurricane that ravaged Galveston, Texas, and left thousands dead was, in one author's words, "a tempest so terrible that no words can adequately describe its intensity."[1] Written and oral accounts by its survivors provide a permanent record of their horror at the carnage they witnessed, as well as their harrowing escapes from the clutches of the storm.

Galveston's Rosenberg Library, long noted for its fine archives of local and early Texas history, holds many accounts of the storm. Some were recorded in the days and months immediately following the disaster; others were put down after many years had passed. The letters, memoirs, and oral histories that follow allow the survivors to tell—in their own words—what they witnessed and experienced during the worst recorded natural disaster ever to befall the United States.

It seems only natural to reproduce these accounts in their original form with only slight editing. Authors often use quotations from original documents selectively to support or disprove their points. Presenting the words of the survivors as they recorded them allows readers the opportunity to make their own judgments and form their own opinions. The vivid descriptions recorded here stand as stark testimony to the enormity of the disaster.

The days leading up to the storm are chronicled in a daily journal kept by Isaac M. Cline, the local U.S. Weather Bureau meteorologist. This official record also follows weather developments after the storm.

As the survivors reflected on their lives and experiences, they put their feelings down on paper in the form of letters to loved ones recalling what they had witnessed. By writing those letters, they not only achieved a catharsis to help them deal with the stunning events, but also left documentary record of the event for future generations.

The oral history recordings were made in the 1960s and 1970s when the survivors were nearing the end of their lives. The accounts are presented here in edited form to make them more readable. Unfortunately, the printed word can only hint at the emotions behind the spoken words. The reader is unable to hear the voice that softened to barely a whisper when describing a mother's despair, or a narrator's last painful memory of a sister who perished after handing over her youngest child. The editors decided to correct minor spelling and grammatical errors that would only serve to distract the reader (e.g., replacing the word "staid" with the correct spelling "stayed"). However, all words remain as they appear in the original accounts—including terms for African Americans that today are considered improper—in the interests of historical accuracy.

For those readers not familiar with Galveston, the streets are laid out in a grid pattern. North–south streets are numbered sequentially beginning in the east, while east–west streets are lettered sequentially beginning at the bay. Lettered streets north of Broadway also have common names; for example, Avenue B is better known as the Strand. We have made every attempt to remain consistent, substituting the lettered names for common names to help the reader get a feel for the location. Maps in each section show where the author was located during the storm.

The idea for this project first came about in September, 1997, when the city and researchers expressed interest in the upcoming centennial anniversary of the 1900 storm. The staff at the Rosenberg Library's Galveston and Texas History Center fielded many questions relating to the various primary manuscript sources held there. Assistant Archivist Shelly Henley Kelly began reorganizing and transcribing oral history interviews never before used by researchers.

In December, 1997, Kelly approached Casey Edward Greene, head of Special Collections, about working on a published collection of the library's 1900 storm manuscript and oral history holdings. She transcribed and researched each account in order to write the commentary and footnotes. Greene painstakingly edited her work by comparing the original handwritten version to the typed copy. He also composed the introduction.

This book would not have been possible without generous support and encouragement from numerous individuals: Nancy Milnor, executive director of the Rosenberg Library, who authorized this project; our coworkers Anna B. Peebler and Julia Dunn, who tirelessly listened to conversation after conversation about the storm; and our families, who supported us in more ways than one, including Marilyn Maniscalco

Henley, who repeatedly trekked to the Texas State Library to search for names on the 1900 Soundex.

Other individuals aided us in the fact-checking process. They are: Mark Martin, Houston Metropolitan Research Center, Houston Public Library; Sharon Perry Martin, Dallas Public Library; and Henry Boening, superintendent of the Galveston Independent School District, and his staff.

Finally, we owe our gratitude to all the survivors who wrote down or told their stories and donated them to the Rosenberg Library for historical preservation and scholarly research.

Through a Night of Horrors

Introduction

The advent of the twentieth century saw Galveston in the midst of an economic boom. In 1899 it was the "third richest city in the United States in proportion to population."[1] This community of 37,789 had good reason for optimism. By 1900, thanks to the efforts of the Galveston Wharf Company, the city had emerged as a deepwater port serving the Texas interior and states west of the Mississippi River. Its wharves, grain elevators, and storage facilities had been developed during the 1890s. The jetties protecting the harbor entrance from an accumulation of sandbars were completed in 1898 with the expenditure of $8.7 million in federal funds.[2]

All major Texas railroads served Galveston. Colis P. Huntington, founder of the Southern Pacific Railroad, selected it for his railway's eastern terminus. In 1899 Southern Pacific purchased and began development of 203 acres along the waterfront. Galveston handled over 60 percent of the state's cotton crop in 1896–97 and again in 1897–98. It was the nation's leading cotton port in 1898–99, although it fell to second place behind New Orleans the next year. In 1899–1900, it ranked third nationally in the export of wheat, sixth in cattle, and seventh in corn.[3] Galveston was also a major banking center. Its burgeoning economy was evident through local improvements in residences, streets, the streetcar system, fire department, and water supply. The federal government aided in the boom by building military fortifications on Galveston Island and at Port Bolivar.[4]

However, its vulnerable location on the Gulf of Mexico placed Galveston directly in the path of an advancing hurricane. In earlier decades, two devastating hurricanes sealed the fate of Indianola, another Texas city located farther down the coast. In September, 1875, a severe hurricane passed over Cuba and headed west-northwest across the Gulf toward Texas. On September 14, 1875, the waters of Matagorda Bay began to rise. Two days later the storm's full fury struck Indianola, destroying three-fourths of the city and claiming approximately three hundred victims.[5] A second hurricane hit Indianola on August 20, 1886, claiming its remnants. Having had their fill of storms, the remaining inhabitants decided to abandon their city.[6]

Despite Indianola's fate, Galveston's residents continued to believe they were impervious to a devastating hurricane; plans to build a seawall to protect the city were discussed but had not come to fruition by 1900. Galveston's brush with disaster came on September 8, 1900. The Storm's death toll, never precisely calculated, was estimated at six thousand or more. The city's financial losses stood at $28 million, including half of its taxable property. Some fifteen hundred acres of shoreline were swept clean. Thousands of houses, the wharves, railroad bridges, and telegraph connections to the outside world were lost.[7]

The decision to rebuild called for major changes. The first requirement was a thorough reorganization of local government. Galveston was heavily in debt, so there was a great need for a more efficient and effective form of governance than the mayor and aldermanic board that traditionally served its residents. The city commission form of government, which featured a mayor and a board of commissioners, was adopted in Galveston on September 18, 1901. It placed responsibility for the delivery of services in the hands of commissioners who headed the city's departments. One commissioner was in charge of finance and revenue; another, the waterworks and sewerage. Two other commissioners were responsible for streets and public property and the police and fire departments respectively. The mayor and city commissioners were elected for two-year terms.

The city commission plan was especially attractive because it was streamlined and established clear lines of responsibility. Another desirable feature was that the local government rested in the hands of seasoned administrators. The mayor and commissioners met together weekly as a board to expedite the city's business, free as much as possible from politics and discord.[8]

In September, 1901, the City Commission and the County Commissioners Court appointed a board of three engineers to make recommendations concerning plans to protect the city from future hurricanes. The Engineering Board included Henry M. Robert, the chairman, and Alfred Noble and Henry Clay Ripley.[9] They issued their first report in January, 1902, calling for the construction of a seventeen-foot-high seawall, the elevation of the city's grade all the way to the seawall, and the creation of an embankment on top of the fill.[10]

In March, 1902, Galveston County voters approved a proposition to issue $1.5 million in bonds for the construction of a seawall. Work commenced in October, and the initial portion was completed in July. This part, which ran over three miles, traversed the island at Sixth Street and extended from Sixth to Thirty-ninth Street. The U.S. Congress authorized the construction of a second portion of the seawall to protect Fort Crockett; this portion started at Thirty-ninth Street and ended at Fifty-third Street. This portion was begun in December, 1904, and completed ten months later.[11]

At the time of the 1900 storm, Galveston stood at a maximum elevation of only 8.7 feet above sea level. In accordance with the Engineering Board's recommendation, the city's surface had to be raised in a sloping manner from behind the seawall to the bay side. This required raising buildings in an area forty blocks long and placing fill beneath them. In January, 1903, the Texas legislature approved a grade-raising bill that authorized the state to donate state taxes collected from Galveston County to the city of Galveston for a period of fifteen years. The contractor, Goedhart and Bates, was a German company. Work commenced behind the seawall in July, 1904. Dredges removed a slurry of sand and water from Galveston Bay and pumped it beneath the structures as the dredges made their way along a canal dug across the city. Residents walked on elevated sidewalks made of planks. New trees had to be planted and new streets paved. In July, 1910, the original portion of the grade-raising contract was completed at a cost of over $2 million.[12]

Galveston stood at a crossroads after the storm. While its residents were absorbed with the recovery process, major developments were taking place elsewhere. The Spindletop oil boom near Beaumont in 1901 and the opening of the Houston Ship Channel in 1914 presaged Houston's economic growth. Galveston also lacked transportation links. A causeway carrying railroads, the interurban, and automobiles to the mainland, was not opened until 1912. Galveston Island's size limited the city's ability to grow. Other cities, such as Houston, Dallas, and San Antonio, developed as transportation centers and enjoyed closer proximity to the state's agricultural hinterlands.[13] The seawall proved its soundness in subsequent hurricanes, including a major storm in August, 1915 (whose intensity exceeded that of the 1900 storm), Hurricane Carla in 1961, and

Hurricane Alicia in 1983. Today, Galveston is a leading tourist destination offering miles of beaches and fishing. Yet with the advent of hurricane season annually, wary eyes cast their gaze toward the Gulf of Mexico. Galveston continues to face the possibility—however slim—of another devastating storm whose toll may equal or exceed that of the 1900 storm.

Over the past century, the 1900 storm has captured the interest of authors. Published works on the hurricane are of several distinct genres produced in different periods. The first months after the storm saw a number of hastily prepared, rambling, and lurid accounts rushed into print with the intent of cashing in while the nation's attention was focused on the cataclysm. These were filled with extensive quotations from accounts by newspaper reporters and testimony of survivors. From a modern perspective, they are perhaps most remarkable for reflecting the racial bigotry of their day. In *Galveston: The Horrors of a Stricken City,* journalist Murat Halstead characterized the city's African American population as lawless, undisciplined, and deceitful.[14] He claimed that fifty individuals were executed for desecrating the dead.[15] Even more salacious was *The Great Galveston Disaster,* whose author, Paul Lester, repeated assertions that ninety African Americans were executed for despoiling corpses and that blacks were guilty of looting.[16]

The tremendous loss of life and terrible devastation, which were real enough and shared by all citizens of Galveston regardless of their color, did not need embroidering. In response to these lurid accounts, Clarence Ousley, editor of the *Galveston Tribune,* edited *Galveston in 1900.* His book was not intended "to appeal to morbid tastes."[17] Instead, it presented an overview of the city's business, educational, governmental, religious, and cultural institutions as well as the effects the storm had on each. *Galveston in 1900* was the product of many contributors, including Rev. James M. Kirwin of Saint Mary's Cathedral and Rabbi Henry Cohen of Temple B'nai Israel, both of whom were prominent in the local relief effort, as well as Ben C. Stuart of the *Galveston Daily News.* It earned the endorsement of the city's mayor, Walter C. Jones, and Texas governor Joseph D. Sayers.

The second genre of writings about the 1900 storm came decades later. It included narratives authored by John Edward Weems and Herbert Molloy Mason, Jr. Weems, an assistant professor of journalism at Baylor University in Waco, Texas, claimed that his *A Weekend in September* was the first book to be written about the storm since 1901. Eschewing earlier publications as much as possible, he drew heavily from personal accounts by survivors and utilized several archives, including the Rosenberg Library's. (His work papers for *A Weekend in September* are preserved at the Rosenberg Library.) Weems dispelled some of the myths that arose after the hurricane, such as the number of looters killed. Herbert Malloy Mason, Jr., a freelance author, wrote *Death from the Sea: Our Greatest Natural Disaster, The Galveston Hurricane of 1900*. Unlike Weems, he consulted books and periodicals about the storm, including Halstead's and Lester's sensational accounts.

Yet another genre, critical assessments of the hurricane and its aftermath, has emerged in conjunction with the centennial of the 1900 storm. This category is exemplified by Erik Larson's *Isaac's Storm: A Man, a Time, and the Deadliest Hurricane in History*. Larson, a contributor to *Time*, centered his account on U.S. Weather Bureau meteorologist Isaac Cline. Cline believed that Galveston was capable of weathering a devastating hurricane and that the shallow waters along the city's beaches would dampen the effects of an approaching storm.[18] In preparing *Isaac's Storm*, Larson utilized many of the Rosenberg Library's manuscript accounts of the hurricane. He likened Galveston to Atlantis as it slipped beneath the waters from the Gulf of Mexico and Galveston Bay.[19]

The accounts by Storm survivors that follow are dramatic evidence of the thoughts and actions of ordinary people caught up in extraordinary circumstances. Unwilling participants in the calamity, they were in the wrong place at the wrong time. Their words, which are remarkable for their sometimes passionate, other times detached—almost clinical—tone, illustrate firsthand the ways in which people respond collectively to cataclysms. Individuals tend to act in characteristic ways during and after a catastrophe. In the emergency phase, they try to flee or escape the threat. When flight is impossible, they seek protection and attempt to protect their loved ones, friends, and neighbors. They try to be with their families. They display heroism. Panic, however, is an uncommon response to disasters.[20]

In the following accounts, Louisa Christina Rollfing describes protecting her daughter against the driving rain as they made their way across the city. Louise Hopkins remembers her mother trying to protect her by keeping her indoors in the storm's aftermath. One of the Rosenberg Library's most poignant accounts is a letter whose author is unknown. It was probably written by a nurse at John Sealy Hospital at the height of the storm. As night drew near and the danger became greater, she reached out through her words to her loved ones.

As soon as the emergency passes, survivors often notice that silence blankets their surroundings. Then they attend to the injured, engaging in rescue work well before the arrival of trained workers. Directing their attention and actions toward others helps them take charge of the situation. If separated from their loved ones, they immediately search for them.[21] These behaviors also manifested themselves in 1900 storm accounts. The hurricane wiped out familiar signposts that gave meaning and definition to the daily lives of Galveston's residents. Family and friends, pets, buildings, neighborhoods, necessities, amenities—all had disappeared into the raging Gulf waters. The huge death toll and destruction were almost impossible to comprehend.

Shocked by what they have seen and experienced, survivors may suppress their feelings or behave inappropriately.[22] Alluding to what has been termed "psychic numbing,"[23] Winifred Black reported that the survivors were "stunned with the merciful bewilderment which nature always sends at such a time of sorrow." Eleanor Hertford spoke of their benumbed state. Lloyd Fayling described the "crazy men and women [who] walked up and down the streets crying and weeping at the top of their voices." Survivors also engage in the "milling process" as they grope for meaning.[24] Ida Smith Austin found meaning in their desire to rebuild; they were literally "picking up the pieces" and moving on with their lives. Others sought meaning in the physical ties they had to the storm. Arnold R. Wolfram describes cutting down a tree in which he had taken refuge so he could claim it as a souvenir.

Furthermore, survivors are changed as a result of their experiences. Grief is a normal reaction to the loss of loved ones. Guilt is prevalent because survivors may wonder why they lived when others died.[25] They express helplessness and a need to explain what has happened. During the post-disaster period they seek to release stress. They respond in psychosomatic ways by developing sweating, tremors, exhaustion, and other symptoms. These symptoms can manifest themselves over a longer term. A calamity can leave its survivors in a heightened state of alertness.[26]

In coping with their experiences and losses, survivors often develop "post-traumatic reactions." They relive their brushes with death by ruminating about their experiences or altogether denying them. These responses sometimes progress into "post-traumatic stress disorder." Rather than subside, symptoms of irritability and anger persist.[27] Five days after the storm, Walker W. Davis wrote his mother about his "shattered nerves."

Many years later, Emma Beal recalled having nightmares after witnessing the burning of bodies.

Death imagery is abundant in 1900 storm accounts. The hurricane left the city strewn with wreckage and thousands of bodies. Funeral pyres burned for days after the storm. These and other elements—such as the heat, mud, slime, and stench—added to the scene's hellish nature. A particularly striking feature of Galveston's ruined landscape was a huge ridge of debris that traversed the city and concealed hundreds of bodies. It is mentioned in Joseph Henry Hawley's letter and Louisa Christina Rollfing's memoir.

Death—on a massive scale and individually—was observable everywhere in Galveston in the days following the storm. John Blagden wrote of wagons passing by carrying bodies. Charles W. Law recalled seeing the bodies of mothers holding their dead babies. Harry Maxson remembered burying the bodies of a woman and her two small children with the help of another man whose name he never learned.

The rumor mill thrives in the wake of a disaster, and rumors abound in the absence of an official explanation of the calamity. Their value lies in helping survivors come to terms with their circumstances.[28] John D. Blagden wrote to his family about rumors concerning persons being executed for desecrating victims and the possibility of famine. The rumors of mass executions were believed, despite the efforts of journalists such as Clarence Ousley and Ben Stuart to dispel them. They persisted even in the survivors' later years—testimony to the degree to which they were believed.

Survivors learn to cope with their experiences and losses by writing about them, speaking about them, or looking toward the future.[29] The following 1900 accounts undoubtedly had therapeutic value in helping them cope with what they experienced. The powerful imagery was shared by all, yet it still was intensely personal. Years later, some survivors would recall images of horror and destruction, testimony to the drama of the events that terrible day in September, 1900, whereas others saw hope and salvation in the tragedy. In view of Galveston's resurgence in the years following the hurricane, Ida Smith Austin expressed perhaps the most profound meaning: "As the oak sinks its roots more deeply and grows more rugged by the storms which seek its destruction so out of this dread experience shall Galveston grow to great strength and greater influence."

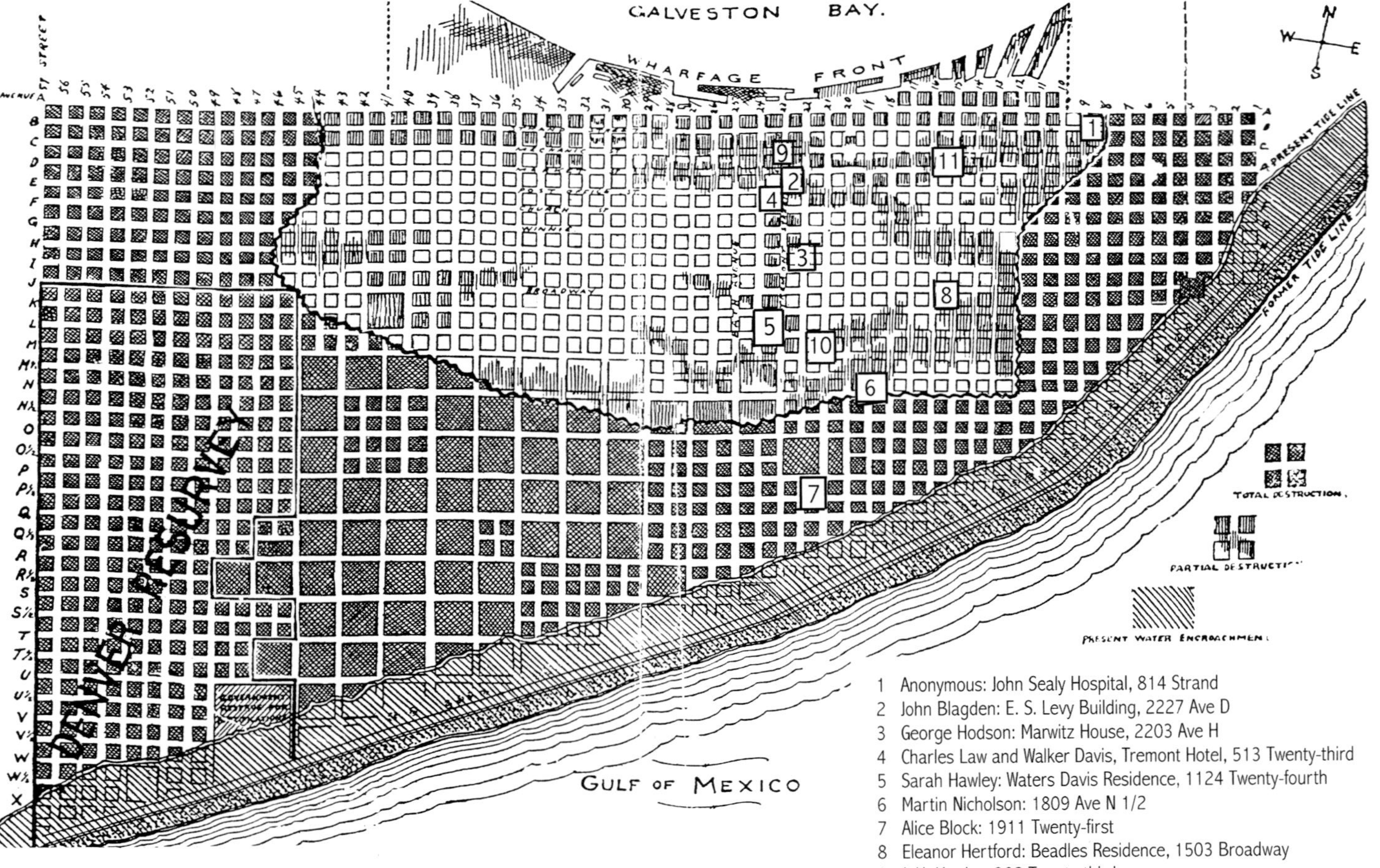

1 Anonymous: John Sealy Hospital, 814 Strand
2 John Blagden: E. S. Levy Building, 2227 Ave D
3 George Hodson: Marwitz House, 2203 Ave H
4 Charles Law and Walker Davis, Tremont Hotel, 513 Twenty-third
5 Sarah Hawley: Waters Davis Residence, 1124 Twenty-fourth
6 Martin Nicholson: 1809 Ave N 1/2
7 Alice Block: 1911 Twenty-first
8 Eleanor Hertford: Beadles Residence, 1503 Broadway
9 J. H. Hawley: 302 Twenty-third
10 James Brown: SW corner 21st Street and Ave L
11 Ida Smith Austin: 1503 Ave C

Survivor Letters

Tuesday, September 4, 1900
U.S. Weather Bureau Report
Nimbus, cumulus, strato-cumulus and alto-stratus clouds. Fresh to brisk easterly winds. Light rain. Heavy rain. Thunderstorm. Advisory message stating "Tropical disturbance moving northward over Cuba" was received and distributed at 5:00 p.m.

Wednesday, September 5
U.S. Weather Bureau Report
Scattered nimbus, strato-cumulus and cumulus clouds. Fresh easterly winds. Light rain. The following advisory message was received and distributed at 11:20 a.m. "Disturbance central near Key West moving northwest. Vessels bound for Florida and Cuban ports should exercise caution as storm likely to become dangerous."

Thursday, September 6
U.S. Weather Bureau Report
Scattered cumulus, strato-cumulus and alto-stratus clouds. Fresh northerly winds. Advisory message in regard to tropical storm central over southern Florida received and distributed at 2:59 p.m.

Friday, September 7
U.S. Weather Bureau Report
Broken cumulus and strato-cumulus clouds. Fresh to brisk northerly winds. Special observations taken at noon and 3:00 p.m. Order to hoist

storm flag northwest 10:35 a.m. received at 11:30 a.m. and hoisted at 11:35 a.m. Rough sea with heavy southeast swells during afternoon and evening.

Saturday, September 8
U.S. Weather Bureau Report
Strato-cumulus and nimbus clouds. Fresh to high northerly winds. Gale of 84 miles an hour from the northeast at 6:15 p.m. when anemometer blew away. Higher wind after this time probably reaching 110 or 120 miles per hour. Special observations taken at noon and 3:00 p.m. Order to change northwest storm warning to northeast at 10:30 a.m. received at 11:10 a.m. and warning northeast hoisted at 11:15 a.m. Warning only remained up a few hours until it was blown down. Instrument shelter with instruments blown down. All instruments not yet found.

Light rain began at 6:45 p.m. and continued into the night; rain gage blown down and record lost, amount up to 3:30 p.m. 1.37 inches. Exceptionally heavy rain after this time continuing into the night. Impossible to obtain records of instruments on roof for p.m. observation as they had blown down. Conditions were also dangerous to approach of roof as entrance was a partial wreck and gave way soon after observation time.

The following special barometer readings were taken during the rapid fall during the late afternoon. The lowest barometer apparently occurred between the two last observations when the barometer stood at about 28.44. The barometer began rising at about 8:30 p.m. and rose about as rapidly as it had fallen.

The tide commenced coming in over low portions of city in early morning and the following telegram was sent at about 7:00 a.m.: "Unusually heavy swells from southeast, intervals one to five minutes overflowing low places south portion city three to four blocks from beach. Such high water with opposing winds never observed previously." The tide continued to rise all day. A sudden rise of 4 feet occurred at 7:30 p.m.

The entire city was under water from 8 to 15 feet deep at 8:00 p.m. The entire south, east and west portions of the city from one to five blocks inland are swept clean, not a house remaining. Many other houses blown down over the city and all other buildings damaged more or less.

Many men, women and children drowned, some entire families, and the number of persons killed or drowned will probably reach more than 5,000 when all reports are received. The streets are one mass of debris and it will be many days before all the dead bodies can be found. Many lives were saved after floating on the drifting debris for several hours. Thousands of people were injured by flying timbers while endeavoring to save themselves.

The damage to property is estimated at $80,000,000.00. The tide began to fall slowly at about 11:00 p.m. and comparatively no damage resulted after this time. I. M. Cline Local Forecast Official and Joseph L. Cline, Observer badly injured in wreck and drift, begin on and among drifting houses from 7:30 to 10:30 p.m.

ANONYMOUS

On September 8, as the storm was beginning, a young woman employed at John Sealy Hospital began writing the exceptionally rare unsigned letter that follows. It is the only account held by the Rosenberg Library known to have been written while the storm was taking place.

A.M.
It does not require a great stretch of imagination to imagine this structure a shaky old boat out at sea. The whole thing rocking like a reef, surrounded by water, said water growing closer, ever closer. Have my hands full quieting nervous, hysterical women.

12-noon.

Things beginning to look serious. Water up to the first floor in the house, all over the basement of the hospital. Cornices, roofs window lights blinds flying in all directions.

Noon.

The scenes about here are distressing. Everything washed away. Poor people trying, vainly to save their bedding, & clothing. Methinks the poor nurses will be trying to save their beds in short order. Now flames in the distance. It is all a grand, fine sight. Our beautiful Bay, a raging torrent.

3 p.m.

Am beginning to feel a weakening desire for something "to cling to." Should feel more comfortable in the embrace of your arms. You hold yourself in readiness to come to us? should occasion demand?

Darkness is overwhelming us, to add to the horror. Dearest—I—reach out my hand to you. my heart—my soul.

1. John Sealy Hospital. "It does not require a great stretch of imagination to imagine this structure a shaky old boat out at sea."—Anonymous

Sunday, September 9
U.S. Weather Bureau Report
Broken stratus, nimbus, strato-cumulus, alto-stratus and cirrus clouds during the day. High subsiding to brisk southerly winds; record lost until 8:00 a.m.; highest velocity estimated at 50 miles or more from the south in early morning.

The rain of yesterday ended sometime in early morning and time unknown; record lost but amount up to 3:30 p.m. of 8th was 1.27 inches. Light scattered showers during the day but beginning and endings unknown; no rain gage and amount of rain, also, unknown.

The tide had receded so that the high places of the city were dry this morning. Low places still covered with water tonight but tide almost normal. All office force reported at office today except Mr. T. C. Bornkessell, Printer. Time of beginning and endings of rain could not be obtained today on account of being where no time could be ascertained. Observations were made as complete as was possible considering the loss of instruments. Thermograph found and put in working order but mechanism of same injured.

No letters, if written, survived to document the day following the storm. According to many of the following accounts, it dawned with a beautiful sunrise, a sharp contrast to the horrors of the night before. Galveston residents, dazed and stunned, emerged from the wreckage and quickly became occupied with what needed to be done to survive.

Monday, September 10
U.S. Weather Bureau Report
Broken cumulus, nimbus and cirrus clouds. Fresh southerly winds prevailed. Light rain from 12:40 p.m. to 12:50 p.m., amount trace.

I. M. Cline, Local Forecast Official, absent today on account of injuries received in storm. Joseph L. Cline, Observer, left in charge but unable to do much. Mr. Ernest E. Kuhnel, Map Distributor absent today on account of looking for bodies of his relatives. Mr. T. C. Bornkessell, Printer, still missing.

Rain gage No. 750 temporarily erected today. A temporary instrument shelter was erected from pieces of old shelters and other pieces of lumber and the following instruments were put up today: Maximum thermometer No. 5148, minimum No. 5635, dry No. 3082 and wet No. 3647. Sunshine recorder can not be found.

JOHN D. BLAGDEN

John D. Blagden wrote to his family in Duluth, Minnesota, while serving a temporary assignment at the Galveston Weather Bureau office away from his permanent station in Memphis, Tennessee. The Blagden family returned his letter to the U.S. Weather Bureau in 1946. The Weather Bureau recognized the importance of preserving the letter and donated it to the Rosenberg Library.

Aside from Isaac Cline's personal report, Blagden's letter is the only other account at the Rosenberg Library of someone stationed at the Weather Bureau office. He recalls both the warning the office received about the storm and what precautions it took across the city.

To All at home

Very probably you little expect to get a letter from me from here but here I am alive and without a scratch. That is what few can say in this storm swept City. I have been here two weeks, to take the place of a man who is on a three months leave, after which I go back to Memphis.

Of course you have heard of the storm that passed over this place last Friday night, but you cannot realize what it really was.[1] I have seen many severe storms but never one like this. I remained in the office all night.[2] It was in a building that stood the storm better than any other in the town, though it was badly damaged and rocked frightfully in some of the blasts. In the quarter of the city where I lodged (south part) everything was swept and nearly all drowned. The family with whom I roomed were all lost. I lost every thing I brought with me from Memphis and a little money, but I think eighty Dollars will cover my entire loss: I am among the fortunate ones.

The Local Forecast Official, Dr. Cline, lives in the same part of the City and his brother (one of the observers here) boarded with him.[3] They did not fare so well. Their house went with the rest and were out in the wreckage nearly all night. The L O F [Dr. Cline] lost his wife but after being nearly drowned themselves they saved the three children. As soon as possible the next morning after the waters went down I went out to the south end to see how they fared out there. I had to go through the wreckage of buildings nearly the entire distance (one mile) and when I got there I found everything swept clean. Part of it was still under water.

I could not even find the place where I had been stopping. One that did not know would hardly believe that that had been a part of the city twenty-four hours before. I could not help seeing many bodies though I was not desirous of seeing them. I at once gave up the family with whom I stopped as lost which has proved true as their bodies have all been found, but the Clines I had more confidence in in regard to their ability to come out of it. I soon got sick of the sights out there and returned to the office to put things in order as best I could. When I got to the office I found a note from the younger Cline telling me of the safety of all except the Drs. wife. They were all badly bruised from falling and drifting timber and one of the children was very badly hurt and they have some fears as to her recovery.

2. U.S. Weather Bureau office in the E. S. Levy Building. "I remained in the office all night. It was in a building that stood the storm better than any other in the town."—John Blagden

Mr. Broncasiel, our printer, lives in another part of the town that suffered as badly is still missing and we have given him up as lost.[4] There is not a building in town that is uninjured. Hundreds are busy day and night clearing away the debris and recovering the dead. It is awful. Every few minutes a wagon load of corpses passes by on the street.

3. *". . . I found everything swept clean. Part of it was still under water."*
—John Blagden

The more fortunate are doing all they can to aid the sufferers but it is impossible to care for all. There is not room in the buildings standing to shelter them all and hundreds pass the night on the street. One meets people in all degrees of destitution. People but partially clothed are the rule and one fully clothed is an exception. The City is under military rule and the streets are patrolled by armed guards.

They are expected to shoot at once anyone found pilfering. I understand four men have been shot today for robbing the dead. I do not know how true it is for all kind of rumors are afloat and many of them are false. We have neither light, fuel or water. I have gone back to candles. I am now writing by candlelight.

A famine is feared, as nearly all the provisions were ruined by the water which stood from six to fifteen feet in the streets and all communication to the outside is cut off.

For myself, I have no fear. I sleep in the office, have food to last for some time and have water, and means of getting more when it rains as it frequently does here and besides I have made friends here who will not let me starve. We had warning of the storm and many saved themselves by seeking safety before the storm reached here. We were busy all day Thursday answering telephone calls about it and advising people to prepare for danger. But the storm was more severe than we expected.

Dr. Cline placed confidence in the strength of his house. Many went to his house for safety as it was the strongest built of any in that part of the town, but of the forty odd who took refuge there less than twenty are now living.

I have been very busy since the storm and had little sleep but I intend to make up for sleep tonight. I do not know how or when I can send this but will send it first chance. Do not worry on my account.

Write soon.
Yours truly
John D. Blagden

Tuesday, September 11
U.S. Weather Bureau Report
Scattered cumulus and strato-cumulus clouds. Fresh easterly winds. I. M. Cline, Local Forecast Official, still unable for duty. Mr. T. C. Bornkessell, Printer, still absent.

GEORGE HODSON

George Hodson—a stenographer with the insurance firm of Beers, Kenison, and Company—sent this letter to his wife, Alice Minot Hodson, who had taken their five-year-old daughter, Rebecca, to visit family out of town. Hodson also mentions that the city had ample warning of the impending storm but failed to take proper precautions. At the end of his letter is the first of many warnings to loved ones to stay out of the city during this terrible time.

My Dear Girl:

I will begin by saying I am alive and unscratched. This letter is a copy of some shorthand notes I made on Sunday morning so you may take everything as of Sunday's date until I mention otherwise.

As you will remember I promised you a long letter on Sunday, but I never dreamed I would have to write you of the serious of affairs resulting from wind and rain which Galveston has been the victim of since Saturday morning. However, I thank God I am well and sound and so are Mrs. Robinson and Miss Kate.[5] It is such a story of wreck, ruin, and loss of life that I hardly know where to begin first.

The weather bureau predicted a severe storm, coming from Cuba and West Indies, on Thursday, but the first indications we had came on Saturday morning when people coming in town from the beach reported that the water was as far as Ave M on Center [Twenty-first] Street and that the streetcars had quit making the circuit. This high water came from the Southeast, which about dinner time changed to Northeast, and this raised the water in the bay until it was over a foot deep in our office before 3 o'clock in the afternoon. I got to dinner all right but never got back nearer the office than Adoue and Lobits Bank and there I stood for two solid hours.[6]

Just about this time I saw John piloting Kenison[7] from the office to where I was, they having had to abandon the office, and as there was no way to get home except walking Vieno[8] and myself took charge of him and started towards his home and waded waist deep, and by the time we got to his house we were all pretty well played out. This was probably about 5 o'clock and after a little strong refreshment and rest Vieno and I started back to town, he to go home and I to Mrs. Robinson's.

We found it an easy job taking Kenison home compared to getting back to town as the wind was then dead against us, and at one time, just as we reached the esplanade on Broadway, the wind got the better of us and we threw ourselves flat on the grass. Finally I reached the Robinsons' and found them getting ready to leave the house, which I persuaded them not to do and go to the Marwitz house on the corner, but I was afterwards sorry I did not let them go, as I finally had to take them to the brick house, and this was one of the most serious and dangerous tasks I have ever had to undertake.[9]

I kept persuading them that the water surely could not rise much higher, but just after dark the water got so high that we could only see the fence, so we decided it was time to move. Fortunately the colored man living in the yard stayed with them, and with his assistance we carried Mrs. R. from her gallery to the front door of the Wylie house, and after getting her in, returned for Miss Kate and finally succeeded in getting her there too. Of course as you may suppose after taking [Kenison] home, I did not have a dry stitch on me, and after taking care of Mrs. R. and Miss Kate you may possibly [guess] my condition. I got to my room about 7 o'clock on Sunday morning.

Mrs. R. and Miss Kate returned to their own house then and found that the water had risen over a foot above the floor. The[y] at once took up all the matting and scraped the worst of the mud off the floor. I thank God you were not here as I do not know what I would have done for the worst is not yet told.

The spectacle on Tremont [Twenty-third] and Market [Avenue D] Streets beggars description. All in the middle of Street was strewn with debris, and there is not a building in the entire [city] but has suffered more

4. Marwitz House. "... go to the Marwitz house on the corner, ... I finally had to take them to the brick house."—George Hodson

5. Corner of Twenty-third Street and Avenue D. "The spectacle on Tremont and Market Streets beggars description."—George Hodson

or less. For instance the entire roof of the Ball School is off, the City hall is one mass of ruins, the Opera House is entirely gone, the First Baptist Church and St. John's Church are each a mass of ruins and so the story goes from one end of town to another, but sadder and more serious still is the great loss of life which is beyond computing. This is something utterly beyond my ability to describe, so I enclose a printed list gotten out today which speaks for itself although it is far from being a complete list.

Now Alice I am happy to say that generally speaking those of our immediate acquaintance have fared not so bad. The Conlons are all safe, though their houses are all more or less damaged, the Shaws are safe, but the house we lived in fell to the ground.[10] Miss Fannie Peacock gets off lightly by losing the tin roof.[11]

I could go on indefinitely describing things but I must stop.

Now my good girl I have to make an appeal to your good sense. This is not a case of quarantine like your Virginia experience. I have told you that I am well and sound, but I must ask you if you have any love whatever for me that you stay where you are and make no effort whatever to come home. I will now close until a more convenient time permits, With love

Affectionately
George

Wednesday, September 12
U.S. Weather Bureau Report
Scattered cumulus and strato-cumulus clouds. Fresh easterly winds. Float self-registering rain gage No. 17 put up and tested out today. I. M. Cline, Local Forecast Official, still unable to report for duty.

CHARLES W. LAW

Charles W. Law, a traveling salesman staying at the Tremont Hotel, wrote this descriptive letter to his wife in Marietta, Georgia. The Tremont Hotel, built in 1872, had about two hundred paying guests at the time of the 1900 storm. Located on Twenty-third (Tremont) Street between Avenues E and F, the five-story brick hotel attracted many people throughout the city who sought shelter. It is estimated that as many as eight hundred to a thousand people crowded the stairways, corridors, and lobby.

Law comments about the oppressive heat and mentions the lack of food and drinking water and how expensive they were to obtain. He shows gratitude for being spared and thinks lovingly of his wife and family. Although he went out into the ruined streets and saw the multitudes of bodies, human and animal, he does not mention how he avoided being drafted to serve with the cleaning crews or how he managed to leave town so quickly.

My own darling -

I have past through the most trying, horrible thing in my life: God knows that on Saturday night at 9 o'clock I had given up all hopes of ever seeing the light of day and my prayers were on my lips asking God to take care of you and the little darling there at home, as it seemed that I would be floating with the thousand poor dead bodies out in the streets at any moment.

As the roof of our hotel had blown off and the bricks and stones were being blown off the building like they were little feathers, the hotel was in total darkness and there were several thousand people in the hotel that came in off the streets for protection and you can't imagine in the least the scene. We were all huddled up in the hall ways, as we could not go into the rooms as the windows were blown through and the plastering in the rooms were all blown down.

I went into my room at 6 o'clock that eve, and both my windows and ceiling [fell] in on me just as I opened the door and it stunned me for the time and I did not dream that I was bruised up so badly until the next morning. I found that my head and shoulders were much impaired and I am now getting so I can do a little writing. My clothes are a sight practically ruined. My sample trunks were damaged very much. They floated around the office of the hotel all night and I had to leave them over in Galveston until there will be some way of getting them out.

I came from Galveston across the Bay to Texas City on a little sail vessel and caught the train there this afternoon for this place in the hot broiling sun and my face is burnt as red as a piece of red flannel! I am feeling just awful! God only knows how I have suffered from the effects of it all. For three days I had only a piece of bread and a cup [of] coffee to eat! Two to three times a day! And had to sleep out in the hallways on the wet carpets and tonight I am thankful to say I have here before me as I write a nice *dry* bed and quite a cool room and I think I will be able to sleep until 9 a.m. tomorrow. Just think we did not have water to drink. I had to go around to the drugstores and pay 25c a pint for mineral waters and it cost me $1.50 a day for water to drink the weather was fearful hot 98° to 99°. Now if I don't have a long spell of fever or rheumatism it will be a miracle. Well this is enough about myself. I will try and give you some little ideas about the scenes of the ill fated City.

6. Tremont Hotel. "As the roof of our hotel had blown off . . . the hotel was in total darkness."—Charles Law

On Sunday morning after the storm was all over I went out into the streets and the most horrible sights that you can ever imagine. I gazed upon dead bodies lying here and there. The houses all blown into pieces; women men and children all walking the streets in a weak condition with bleeding heads and bodies and feet all torn to pieces with glass where they had been treading through the debris of fallen building[s]. And when I got to the gulf and bay coast I saw *hundreds* of houses all destroyed with dead bodies all lying in the ruins, little babies in their mothers arms.

My God! How I did feel for them and thank God for the goodness he has shown unto my little family and how I do love my little family. And then a faint sad stroke came to my heart, does your little wife love as you do her? Only way I answered such in my heart, I hoped she did! As I am truly a devotee! As all the courage of a strong man is made weak when he dwells on things of the kind! Questioning the love of the one whom he has loved from his boyhood.

So I will continue. I went from the shores to the interior of the City

7. "On Sunday morning . . . I went out into the streets. . . . The houses all blown into pieces."—Charles Law

and every step you would take you could see dead bodies of *all kinds*: horses, mules, cats, dogs, chickens and even snakes. The least estimate there is 8 to 10 thousand people killed that lived in Galveston say nothing of the loss of the little towns that are on the coast around the city.

On Monday they took the bodies up and carried them out to sea and buried them there and Tuesday they could not take them up fast enough so they cremated them wherever they run up on them and when I left there today I saw them still at work with hundreds of hands cremating the bodies. None of the bodies the last two days were identified. They could not allow them to do so as the air was foul. Most horrible! Most horrible!

On leaving there today on the sail vessel we saw more bodies than we could count out in the waters. The waters in some places were *black* with bodies and when we got way over across the bay we found the shore full of debris piled up on the dead bodies. Oh! little girl I have been through with more than I can ever tell in helping around among the suffering. I have seen sights that would break the heart of an iron man, but I stuck by them. I am mailing you a paper which will give you some idea. They can't exaggerate the matter at all beyond anything like that. I sent you 3 telegrams I trust you received them all! As I could not use my hand to write. I will be here a week so you can address me *here* your next letter. I will send you my route as soon as I get my trunks.

Kiss our dear little ones for their papa. God bless you all with love from

Your cripple[d] boy
Charlie

8. "*. . . I saw them still at work with hundreds of hands cremating the bodies. . . . Most horrible!"—Charles Law*

SARAH D. HAWLEY

Another person who left Galveston on September 12 was Sarah Davis Hawley with her four-month-old son, Harry Hawley, Jr. Sarah wrote to her parents, Mr. and Mrs. Waters S. Davis, who were vacationing with their two unmarried daughters, Emma and Mary, in Europe. Sarah and her husband, referred to here as "Mr. H.," were staying in the Davis family home at 1124 Twenty-fourth Street, at the corner of Twenty-fourth and Avenue L, while the family was traveling.

Sarah and Harry, Jr. traveled aboard the steamship Mexican *to New Orleans and from there took another ship to New York, where they traveled by train to Litchfield, Connecticut. Mr. Hawley's sister, Mary Willis, whose mother-in-law built what is now known as the Moody Mansion, cared for them until they could return to Galveston.*

Sarah wrote her parents very expressive details about the storm, damage to the house, and her actions to protect their property. One can only imagine the odors around the island from the stinking mud, wet plaster, and overturned outhouses or water closets.

Sarah, writing from aboard the Mexican *while anchored off Galveston, reports on the condition of a great many of their friends, some of whom are mentioned in other letters. She describes the actions of her parents' servants, and mentions that she went around with a pistol to protect herself from looters.*

SEPTEMBER 12

My dear Mother -

This first part was written to Emma some days before the storm.[12] Friday evening the wind was very strong and Saturday morning it was even stronger the sky dark, but otherwise there was nothing unusual. At dinner it looked worse but we weren't at all apprehensive. Mr. H. came home to dinner and went to town afterwards—About four p.m. some one went by and called in that the beach was up to 13th and B'dway [Broadway] and in a very short time it came rushing by our house carrying lumber, barrels and all kind of rubbish. Mr. H. got home about half past four drenched through. We immediately went up into the Attic to place pans to catch the rain.

We, with Richard's help, worked like mad until six, when we gave up

9. Waters Davis residence. "We . . . worked like mad until six, when we gave up trying to keep the house dry."—Sarah Davis Hawley

trying to keep the house dry.[13] It was awful! Slates flying and pounding down the roof, the brick from the chimneys thumping down, the blinds slamming and the skylight sailing off! The rain came down in sheets on the stairs every minute becoming worse all over the house. At six we began to realize our danger as the water was then in the yard and rising fast. We rushed upstairs, flung on our bathing suits, got warm things for son and underwear for the women. When I got down found all of Augusta's family in the kitchen and a strange colored woman—they were half dead with fright and wet through.

Motts' chimneys fell and the iron railing round the top of the house flew into our yard and buried itself in the ground so deep that the next day two men could just pull it up.[14] We stood by the window watching the water rise and waiting every moment for the house to fall. The water reached its highest about half past ten (four feet in the basement) stayed that height some time and then fell rapidly. The wind blew an unheard of gale 94° and then broke the machine on the Cotton Exchange; it was ghastly. We expected to have to rush out any moment into the water but made up our minds to stick to the house until it fell.

About half past six or seven we saw a man on the L street sidewalk; the water was up to his armpits. Then we made him come in and when he got on the gallery he looked like death and couldn't stand steady—the wind being so strong we had to yell to each other. Later we saw a man go by on horse back in the middle of the street, the horse's head alone being out of water—we tried to make him come in but he didn't see us and couldn't hear our calls.

The window blinds in Mary's room were blown off and the window smashed, so in order not to let the wind into the house we had to nail it up with boards from the attic. It was a great task for the only lights we had were pieces of candles and my little candle lamp. We had to throw the boards down the attic stairs for we could hardly keep Mary's door closed even with two men holding it. That is (the window) the only damage done to Mary's room except a few spots on the ceiling. Emma's bed was wet through to the floor and her desk was badly spotted, but I rubbed the spots almost off next day.

In your room that night it was just as it was raining outdoors, but most wonderful to relate your furniture wasn't hurt a particle. It was well covered. The ceiling is wet all over and I fear will soon fall. The east wall is badly cracked and the matting ruined. I had all my work out on your sofa and it was drenched and I fear your sofa is badly injured. The bathroom ceiling is wet all over and the window blinds gone and window broken. The two hall ceilings are wet also Waters old room and the north room upstairs has fully three inches of plaster and water the furniture all wet and warped and one bed very wet—ceiling all most all down.

Down stairs the Parlor and hall are right good, also the sitting room, the north room ceiling is wet and the dining room and hall too—the carpet in the dining room was badly wet. The front kitchen ceiling is wet and the hall between kitchens is gone entirely the back kitchen was wet through and through every pan and kettle wet and all over the floor and in servants room stoves brown with rust and the north wall of room is about six inches from the east wall. Servants room not inhabitable. The house is badly warped.

In the yard all the trees are down except about four or five. The palm in front of dining room still stands. Arbors down one fig tree the closest is fallen almost on top of Buddha who still stands the Lanterns are fallen to pieces but the boy and cat is saved. The stable is standing on the side walk on the top story and everything either broken or out in the air. The palms in lots are standing but my opinion is that everything will die on account of salt water.

But my dear Mother you got off very easily for most people haven't a roof to cover them nor a thing to wear. After the water subsided we saw people go by with nothing on but a blanket or a grain sack. The man we took in was a treasure and worked like a horse you can't realize it but it was life or death that night. Sunday morning we went out as soon as we all had coffee—oh it was ghastly no house whole except Waters', Gresham's, Sealy's and a few others and the deaths—under every fallen house lay the people owning it.[15] We hear horrors every hour too awful to think on.

I had to keep my eyes turned from many a sight. People went by homeless and hungry. We went in to see the Porters and found their house off the piles on the ground full of mud and plaster two inches thick.

The hospital is badly injured and over one hundred patients dead, the schools and churches are all down but the jail is standing firm. The forts are nothing but mounds of dirt, at the camp out at the Denver thirty-five soldiers were lost.[16] Among the missing are Chas. Peek's brother's family—ten of the Harris family—all the Mastersons except May and Reba. Walter Fisher and family—Mr. Ripley's son—Claud Gary lost wife and children.[17] The three Davenport children, Miss Rebecca Harris, Mrs. Heideman's house is no where to be found and she most likely killed.[18] Mr. H. went out to look for her but couldn't find a trace of anything.

Mr. and Mrs. Irving were in the water all night and drifted to safety into the convent. Mrs. I with not a thing on—their house is gone absolutely and they saved nothing. Also the Hadens got off with their lives alone. Charlotte was parted from her baby all night, they saved only the clothes they had on. Mr. Allen and family are lost, the milkman—Ritters saloon fell in and killed Mr. Stanley Spencer, Will Daily, Chas. Kellner, Sr. and Dick Lord. They were drinking and making merry.[19]

Mrs. Kopperl's house is a ruin—roof sliced off and the pillars standing without support. The chimney fell into the dining room and all most killed Nana and family; they had to rush out on the fron[t] gallery and wait there until the water went down.[20]

Mr. Palmer lost wife and child. The Comptons have a ruin for a house also Eichlitz. Mrs. E. had a terrible time in her condition. Hortense Bardash fainted in the water and was rescued at great peril. My old teachers Mr. Borden and Herr Rherman are gone and numberless others that we know—the list so far has reached 5000.

The Captain of this boat says he counted two hundred and then went

10. *". . . Ritters saloon fell in and killed Mr. Stanley Spencer, Will Daily, Chas. Kellner, Sr. and Dick Lord. They were drinking and making merry."* *—Sarah Davis Hawley*

11. *"Mrs. Kopperl's house is a ruin—roof sliced off and the pillars standing without support."—Sarah Davis Hawley*

in to get relief from the horrid sights. The cemetery gave up its dead and animals by the hundreds were drowned. The odors are awful and to cap all the cisterns had salt water in them, ours was like brine, but fortunately for us Mr. Van den Brook had a cistern in the house and gave us water. Ice we had to get from the Brewers. Mr. H and a colored man had to carry 50 lbs. to the house. Fortunately we had some provisions and Mr. H. got a large box of Uneeda biscuits from the factory—milk for son I got at Mrs. Gilberts—she had a little feed saved in the house for her cattle otherwise what would I have done—

The house smelled so of wet plaster and the ceiling falling we had to sleep in the sitting room and the nurse in the back hall as neither the servants room nor kitchen are safe. The basement is filled several inches with mud and the heater of course full of water. The closet is over turned in the yard and the odor is very bad—the upstairs closet backed up and also smells.

The day after the storm we went down early in the morning to see how W. [Waters, Jr.] and D [Daisy] faired and then went down to Mr. H's.[21] On the way met a woman who had lost thirteen [people in her family], all her clothes and house—awful!

At half past twelve I let Nancy go to see what she had left and Augusta went with her husband to find relatives. Mr. H. had to go down town so I had the entire charge of baby and could do nothing towards cleaning the house and was really too dead to attempt anything. Nancy didn't return until eight after we were ready for bed so we had to bring down a mattress pillow etc for her use. She hasn't a sign of a relative and little else than the things at our house which were scarcely hurt at all yet she behaved awfully—wouldn't do a thing towards helping and when I left her with baby she left him as soon as my back was turned. She wanted to see all the horrors and to talk about them in fact was simply daft and behaved as if out of her head.

Monday we all worked hard Mr. H. and Richard downstairs and Augusta and I upstairs. It was a gigantic task and towards the last I had to go round in stocking feet as my feet were so sore and large from being wet so long. Nancy left me again all the afternoon. While I was sitting holding son two colored women passed famished. I gave them what I could and later a young woman came by with a wrapper on and no hat. I gave her your old black straw on the back hall rack and upon inquiry found she had a baby seven weeks old and that she, her mother and father in law had no where to go as their house was a ruin so I told them to come to us. They arrived just before supper and slept in the front hall. They had been up on chairs to their necks in water all night holding the baby on a mattress.

The water was so bad and the odor that Mr. H tried to get us out of town Monday but couldn't. Mr. McVitie sent for him Tuesday while at breakfast and said we could leave on a steamer for N.O. [New Orleans] at eleven. He asked Dr. Sampsons advice and he said take us out immediately.[22] We had just time to throw a few things into a trunk, write Waters a note and fly. We got a dray and went down on it. The boat didn't leave until four, just before then Mr. Crocker and family came down and we decided to go over with them to this boat, the *Mexican.*

When we will sail or where we don't know as the Captain is waiting for orders, but here we have a good air and water and no odor. As we came over the bay was full of dead horses and under the wharf were dead human bodies; it was horrible.

I feel dreadful about the house being left though of course Augusta is in charge, but Mr. H. said you would wish us to leave he felt sure as every one thought we would have fever. They have had to burn quantities of bodies and to bury bodies where they lay in the street and yards. The[y] started by taking 400 out in a barge and throwing them into the Gulf but they drifted back and the stench was horrible.

Mr. Crocker and Mr. H. go on shore every day and work only returning at dark. Yesterday they had nothing at all to eat until their return. Tuesday night son was taken very ill and vomited and gagged all night, no sleep finally we brought him on deck and I was so weary with all my anxiety I could scarcely keep awake. He was all right again yesterday and today is as well as ever. We sleep on deck and I try to keep him out all day. Yesterday several bodies went by but none today. We thought the city was on fire last night, but they were only burning bodies and lumber.

Mr. Spillain is seriously injured in Houston;[23] he was the first to get news to the outside world and in the attempt was considerably hurt. Men every where are ruined and most have lost relatives. Lee Thornton lost his two children. Night before last the Hoodoo's threatened to burn the town for they were made to work without pay. The dead have been frightfully ill treated, robbed ears torn and fingers cut for their jewelry. Thank goodness you all escaped—what will you do?

Mr. H. thinks we had better go on to his sister—leave the baby and

12. Harry Hawley, Jr., and Sarah Davis Hawley Litchfield, Connecticut, October, 1900. "Mr. H. thinks we had better go on to his sister—leave the baby and come back alone."—Sarah Davis Hawley

come back alone or with me if I won't stay. Nothing much can be done now for the town is in such a horrible state.

Richard intended to leave Saturday evening but when the storm came up stayed with us. Monday he informed Mr. H. that he wanted higher wages or would leave. Mr. H. thought it best to keep him and offered him more but I came out and blew Richard sky high and told him not one cent more would he get and that he could leave right away. He immediately turned round and stayed. He behaved very badly the last few days he was there and on Sunday only came back for meals and wouldn't help.

Augusta and her husband were bricks, perfectly invaluable I wish you could give them something. Nancy got so bad that I wouldn't take her with me so my time is fully taken up by baby.

Today washing clothes until my back ached. During the storm in my excitement I moved your chiffonier before the window alone—to keep out the wind that tried me greatly.[24]

Mrs. Compton's baby is very sick from being in the water so long and she is half crazy for they have only the clothes on their back and they are borrowed. They are camping in the Sweeney house.[25]

I am so much worried about the house—do hope you will think we acted wisely and not think us neglectful of your house and things. Tuesday I went round with a pistol as so many people had been killed while trying to protect their things—

Oh you can never realize the awful mess of it all. Why even the jetties are almost gone and the strongest houses ruined. Will end this sorrowful tale and have Mr. H. mail it when he goes in tomorrow. With a heart full of love and hoping soon to hear of your plans.

Lovingly
Sarah

Thursday, September 13
U.S. Weather Bureau Report
Few cumulus, strato-cumulus and cirrus clouds. Light to fresh variable winds. Lightning in the east at 8:20 p.m. and continued into the night. I. M. Cline, Local Forecast Official, still unable to report for duty. Mr. T. C. Bornkessell, Printer, still missing. Several parties have already stated that they saved many lives through the storm on the strength of the information received at this office, some saving as many as five persons.

WINIFRED BLACK

The following report from the New York Journal's *special correspondent, Mrs. Winifred Black, appeared in the program of a benefit concert held in Baltimore, Maryland. The account, written by an outsider who did not experience the storm, views the destruction objectively from a reporters' point of view.*

Articles such as hers appeared across the country as appeals for aid for stricken Galveston. She writes in an almost glorified manner to capture her readers.

I begged, cajoled and cried my way through the line of soldiers with drawn swords who guard the wharf at Texas City and sailed across the bay on a little boat which is making irregular trips to meet the relief trains from Houston.

The engineer who brought our train down from Houston spent the night before groping around in the wrecks on the beach looking for his wife and three children. He found them, dug a rude grave in the sand and set up a little board marked with his name. Then he went to the railroad company and begged them to let him go to work.

The man in front of me on the car had floated all Monday night with his wife and mother on a part of the roof of his little home.[26] He told me that he kissed his wife good-by at midnight and told her that he could not hold on any longer; but he did hold on, dazed and half conscious, until the day broke and showed him that he was alone on his piece of dried wood. He did not even know when the women that he loved had died.

Every man on the train—there were no women there—had lost some one that he loved in the terrible disaster, and was going across the bay to try and find some trace of his family—all except the four men in my party. They were from outside cities—St. Louis, New Orleans, and Kansas City. They had lost a large amount of property and were coming down to see if anything could be saved from the wreck.

They had been sworn in as deputy sheriffs in order to get into Galveston. The city is under martial law, and no human being who cannot account for himself to the complete satisfaction of the officers in charge can hope to get through.

We sat on the deck of the little steamer . . . along the line of the shore there rose a great leaping column of blood-red flame.

"What a terrible fire!" I said. "Some of the large buildings must be burning." A man who was passing the deck behind my chair heard me. He stopped, put his hand on the bulwark and turned down and looked into my face, his face like the face of a dead man, but he laughed.

"Buildings?" he said. "Don't you know what is burning over there? It is my wife and children, such little children; why, the tallest was not as high as this"—he laid his hand on the bulwark—"and the little one was just learning to talk."

13. "The city is under martial law."—Winifred Black

"That's right," said the U.S. Marshal of Southern Texas, taking off his broad hat and letting the starlight shine on his strong face. "That's right. We've had to do it. We've burned over 1,000 people to-day, and to-morrow we shall burn as many more.

"I have been out on inspection all day, and I find that our first estimate of the number of dead was very much under the real. Five thousand would never cover the number of people who died here in that terrible storm.

"I saw my men pulling away some rubbish this very morning right at the corner of the principal street. They thought there might be some one dead person there. They took out fourteen women and three little children. We have only just begun to get a faint idea of the hideous extent of this calamity. The little towns along the coast had been almost completely washed out. We hear from them every now and then as some poor, dazed wretch creeps somehow into shelter and tries to tell his pitiful story. We have only just begun our work.

"The people all over America are responding generously to our appeals for help, and I would like to impress it upon them that what we need now is money, money, money and disinfectants. Tell your people to send all the quick-lime they can get through.[27] I wish I could see a dozen train-loads of disinfectants landed in this city to-morrow morning. What we must fight now is infection, and we must fight it quick and with determination or it will conquer us."

The men of my party came over and took me from the great damp tomb of a room, where I was trying to write, to the Aziola Club across the street.[28] There were eighteen or twenty men there, most representative men of the city of Galveston, rich, influential citizens. They had all been on police duty or rescue work of some sort. The millionaire at the table next to me wore a pair of workmen's brogans, some kind of patched old trousers and a colored shirt much the worse for wear.[29] He had been directing a gang of workmen who were extricating the dead from the fallen houses all day long.

In the short time I have been here I have met and talked with women who saw every one they loved on earth swept away from them out into the storm. I have held in my arms a little lisping boy not eight years old, whose chubby face was set and hard when he told me how he watched his mother die. But I have not seen a single tear. The people of Galveston are stunned with the merciful bewilderment which nature always sends at such a time of sorrow.

As I look out of my window I can see the blood-red flame leaping with fantastic gesture against the sky. There is no wire into Galveston, and I will have to send this message out by the first boat. The Western Union hopes to get its wires through this afternoon. Then I will have the situation better in hand and will be able to tell more definitely just what this brave people, who are trying so courageously to stem the awful tide of misery which has overwhelmed them, need the most.

The people of Galveston are making a brave and gallant fight for life. The citizens have organized under efficient and willing management. Gangs of men are at work everywhere removing the wreckage. The city is districted according to wards, and in every ward there is a relief station. They give out food at the relief stations.

I asked a prominent member of the Citizens' Committee this morning where I should go to see the worst work which the storm had done.[30] He smiled at me a little, pitifully. His house, every dollar he has in the world, and his children, were swept away from him last Sunday night.

"Go?" said he. "Why, anywhere within two blocks of the very heart of the city you will see misery enough in half an hour to keep you awake for a week of sleepless nights."

I went to the heart of the city. I did not know what the names of the streets were or where I was going. I simply picked my way through masses of slime and rubbish which scar the beautiful wide streets of this once beautiful city. The stench from these piles of rubbish is almost overpowering. Down in the very heart of the city most of the dead bodies have been removed, but it will not do to walk far out.

A young man well known in the city shot and killed a Negro who was cutting the ears from a dead woman's head to get her earrings out. The Negro lay in the street like a dead dog, and not even the members of his own race would give him the tribute of a kindly look.

The abomination of desolation reigns on every side. The big houses are dismantled, their roofs gone, windows broken, and the high-water mark showing inconceivably high on the paint. The little houses are gone—either completely gone or they are lying in heaps of kindling wood, covering no one knows what horrors beneath.

The main streets of the city are pitiful. Here and there a shop of some sort is left standing. The merchants are taking their little stores of goods that have been left them and are spreading them out in the bright sunshine. The water rushed through the stores as it did through the houses, in an irresistible avalanche that carried all before it. The wonder is not that so little of Galveston remains standing, but that there is any of it at all.

Every street corner has its story. The eye-witnesses of a hundred deaths have talked to me and told me their heart-rending stories, and not one of them has told of a cowardly death. A woman told me that she and her husband went into the kitchen and climbed upon the kitchen table to get away from the waves, and that she knelt there and prayed. As she prayed the storm came in and carried the whole house away, and her husband with it, and yesterday she went out to the place where her house had been, and there was nothing there but a little hole in the ground.

Her husband's body was found twisted in the branches of a tree half a mile from the place where she last saw him. She recognized him by a locket he had around his neck—the locket she gave him before they were married. It had her picture and a lock of the baby's hair in it. The woman told me all this without a tear or a trace of emotion. No one cries here. They will stand and tell the most hideous stories without the quiver of an eyelid.

14. "Every street corner has its story."—Winifred Black

The hideous horror of the whole thing has benumbed every one who saw it. No one tells the same story of the way the storm arose, or how it went. No man tells the story of his rescue quite alike.

But the city is gradually getting back to a normal understanding of the situation. The Mayor is doing everything in his power to straighten matters out.[31] Martial law is strictly enforced. The chief of police is very, very busy. I like the chief of police of Galveston.[32] He knows his business, and he does not care a thing who likes what he does or who doesn't like it. He is really the force behind the fine organization which is gradually growing into useful life here now in the reconstruction of the city.

There are thousands and thousands of families in Galveston to-day without food or properties or a place to lay their heads. It will take thousands and thousands of dollars to put them on their feet again. I believe that the people of America will see that money is not lacking. But, oh, in pity's name, in America's name, do not delay one single instant. Send this help quickly, or it will be too late.

WINIFRED BLACK

Friday, September 14
U.S. Weather Bureau Report
Stratus clouds. Fresh westerly winds. I. M. Cline Local Forecast Official, still unable to report for duty. Mr. T. C. Bornkessell, Printer still missing. There is now no hope of his return to duty as he was evidently killed or drowned during the storm of September 8, 1900.

MARTIN NICHOLSON

Martin Nicholson, a Scottish immigrant working as a night jailer at the Galveston County Jail, wrote to his wife and twenty-year-old daughter who were staying in Yoakum, Texas. According to his letter, he evidently quit his job after having an argument about an escape.

Nicholson lived with two boarders at 1809 Avenue N ½. One of them, Joe Brokoff, was a Russian immigrant who was a clerk at Gengler Brothers Grocery. Gustav Nagel and his wife, both from Germany, lived next door at 1813 Avenue N ½.

SEPTEMBER 14

My dear Wife and Daughter:

I suppose you got my letter written on Saturday the 8th, in which I told you of the high water, not thinking there was any danger; but by 5 o'clock, when Joe came home, the water was already five feet in the yard and rising rapidly. He tried to take the horses down town for safety; but found the streets on both sides so blocked up with floating timbers of houses to the East and South of us, that he couldn't get through; so he put them in the hall-way of the two-story (Hardie) house.[33]

By the time he got back the water had risen a foot or more—so much that a loose horse was drowning on the sidewalk in front of Nagels. Joe suggested that we should try to go, with the Nagels, to the two-story house it being higher than ours; but I, fortunately, decided to stick to our own house which was the means of saving our lives, as the two-story went to pieces during the night—not a sign of it or the horses to be seen anywhere.

By 8 o'clock the water touched the top step of the steps leading to the back gallery. We then took up the carpet in the parlor and cut two holes in floor—one in the hall, the other in dining room—so as to allow the water to get into the house and by its weight keep the house from being lifted off the supports. But all we could do proved of no avail. We had just got through when the house went off the supports and in less time than I can tell it there was eight feet of water in the house. The rush of water was so sudden and strong that it took me off my feet and I found myself swimming about, not knowing where I was as the lights had gone out.

I heard Joe shouting "come here" but from the roar and noises could not tell where he was. Finally I got near him and he got me by the hand and pulled me onto the lower steps of the attic stairs. We spent [an] anxious night and saved seven lives by pulling them in thro' the East window.

The ruin and desolation is indescribable—the loss of life appalling. We have lost *everything* you may say. Today is the first time I have come down town after some mail that Schirmer told me about.[34] The only one of importance is from my old time friend, Pat Massey, asking me to draw on him *at once* for $10.00 if I need it, telling me to let him know how we are fixed and that his purse though not so "deep as a well nor so wide as a barn door" is at my disposal. This is very kind on his part, don't you think

15. *"The ruin and desolation is indescribable—the loss of life appalling. We have lost* everything *you may say."—Martin Nicholson*

so? I shall write him a nice answer; but shall not avail myself of his offer *at present.* When we get so that can see our way to re-establish ourselves we may find it advisable to call on him for the loan of a fifty or so. Joe has kept me supplied with food—canned meat, bread and a bottle of good whiskey with tobacco and matches—so I am all right you see.

I am in excellent health so far. Being stunned by this overwhelming disaster I lay perfectly idle for the first two days. It then dawned upon me that I might save part of the clothing etc. if I could get water to wash the mud off. The mud! It is six inches thick over everything—a nasty greasy, stinking stuff. The nearest water I know of was the gulf until I discovered a cistern over half full quite close as I thought; but it took me nearly a whole day to cut my way with the ax to find the water to be salt. I have washed some of Joe's and my own clothes for the past two days.

We are located on the north side of N ½ with one house between us and 19th St. I didn't tell you in my letter of the 8th, which you may or may not have got, nor did I intend to tell you till you got back that Henry and I had high words over the escape and that I quit him and came home on Sunday, the 2nd. I knew it would hasten your return so I concluded to say nothing.

Don't let that worry you however. Trouble enough as it is. The city is

16. 1814 Avenue N½. "We are located on the north side of N½."—Martin Nicholson

under martial law. You can go nowhere without a pass. Gus came up on Sunday and found me. I went to his office today and learned that he was sent to Houston two days ago, so I know he has either wired or written you of my safety. Today I got offers of assistance from the K of P. relief committee.[35] The Mason's will likely do something also and money is being subscribed all over the county. Whether we will get our just share is another question, however. *Stay where you are,* you can do no good; but lots of harm by coming back here now. It was a God's blessing you were not here. Don't worry about me. I am all right. *Write soon.* Care the *Peter Gengler Co.*

Your loving husband and father
M. Nicholson

WALKER W. DAVIS

Walker W. Davis appears to be another salesman from out of town who was caught in the wrong place at the wrong time. Along with Charles W. Law, Davis was one of an estimated eight hundred to a thousand people who waited out the storm in the Tremont Hotel. He commented on the serious lack of food and drinking water until he reached the mainland.

Like many tourists today, Davis visited the Gulf during the early stages of the storm to view the large swells. His experiences in Galveston from the storm left him an emotional wreck. He wrote this letter while in San Antonio.

SEPTEMBER 14

My Dear Mother

I know you are anxious to hear from me. Gertie had already telegraphed you before I got home which I fully expected never to do. I was called to Galveston by our chapman and got there Thursday morning.[36] Every thing was beautiful there then Friday evening I went over to the beach and took a Bath in the surf by moonlight—quite a large number of people were there. The extremely heavy swell of the Gulf rather startled me so did not stay in long.

Saturday morning the sky looked very Dark with a slight rain falling, wind blowing about 10 miles an hour. About 11 o'clock I heard that the

17. "I took a [street]car and went down to the Beach."—Walker W. Davis

breakers in the Gulf were wrecking the buildings on the shore. It was raining quite hard then. I took a [street]car and went down to the Beach as I wanted to see how the Gulf looked in a storm. When we reached the trestle that runs out into the water you know where that is; we could go no further as the waves had partially wrecked it. The sight was grand at that time. I watched the waves wash out and break those shell houses, theatres and lunch rooms until I saw that the waves were coming too close for comfort.

I started to go back to town, but found that the streetcars had stopped running this was about 12:30 p.m. The water had then got so high that I had to wade in water above my knees with a driving rain that felt like hail when it struck my face. I was just one hour getting to the hotel. I got my dinner and started out again. As I was already wet through it did not make much difference. I went down to the bay side and watched the storm until four o'clock. The storm was now gradually increasing in fury, the rain was terrible and wind blowing a gale and bringing the waters of the bay over the streets. I stayed there until the water came over the sidewalk. Then I became to be nervous, but never thought of what was to follow.

I walked over Tremont St.—or rather waded as row boats were being used then in the streets to the Tremont Hotel. I was becoming more worried each minute. As darkness came on the terror increased. I could not leave the hotel as it was impossible to live two seconds in that wind and water. The water rose 2½ feet an hour until it stood 3½ feet on the floor of the hotel. You know how high that is from street-level, was then 7 feet in the street. I do not know how we survived through that terrible night. The howl of the wind would be followed by the crashing of buildings. Each minute part of the hotel would give away and crash in. It was the most horrible experience I ever passed through, as we were expecting each minute to be our last.

The sea ran as high in the streets of the town as it did in the Gulf. The wind blew from 120 to 130 miles an hour. There were two thousand in the hotel that night, if it had gone you can guess the rest. One hour more of that wind would have killed every person on the Island.

We all thanked God in the morning that were permitted to see daylight again. I thought of everything—can't describe my thoughts that night. Sunday morning I was afraid to move. Started out three times and came back. When I did muster courage to venture out, what a sight met my gaze. The newspapers cannot describe half and have only given a partial description of the calamity. The Gulf side of the Island was swept clean for six blocks from end to end of the Island. You could not tell that there had ever been a building there. The Bay side was nearly in the same condition, piled high with the wreckage of boats of all kinds.

Dead bodies were everywhere to be seen in all kinds of shapes. Nearly all nude—The wind and water had stripped every vestige of clothing off of them. I had nothing to eat from Saturday noon until Sunday night, not even a drink of water. The full extent of deaths will never be known. It is at least 10,000 if not more. The stench from dead bodies was terrible Sunday morning, but got worse as each day's hot sun found them.

I could not get away from there or get any word out of the Island as all wires were ruined and railroad bridges were gone and only three boats left. The distance to the mainland was 2½ miles so could not swim there. Tuesday at 4 o'clock the Telegraph Co. got a boat to take their men to Virginia Point.[37] That is where the railroads used to cross the bridges. We found hundreds of corpses floating in the bay. When we got to the

18. "The Gulf side of the Island was swept clean for six blocks from end to end."
—Walker W. Davis

mainland we were happy. There was no railroad nearer than seven miles as everything had been washed away.

We all started in and walked part of the time through water up to our waists, but still happy to be alive. After walking over the prairie over dead animals and human bodies we at last reached a relief train that had been sent down as far as they could get from Houston. Two boxcars and two flat cars. When we saw the smoke of the engine two miles distant every one in the party yelled as loud as they could for joy. We reached Houston all right—then came to San Antonio. I have not been able to do anything since my experience in Galveston. Every little noise startles me. My nerves are gone. Will go to work again Monday Sept 17th.

This paper has been through the flood and looks little the worse for wear. I was soaked in salt-water for three days. There are some Utica [New York] people killed in Galveston.

I will send you the papers from here which will give you some idea of [what] has happened it is ten times worse than any newspaper account so far. I was there and know the papers were not. I thought of you [and] Gertie and thanked God you were all safe. I never expected to see any of you again, but I am still on Earth and well except for a few bruises and shattered nerves.

Give my best regards and love to all inquiring friends and lots of love and kisses to you. I have your $20. Carried it through the flood—will send it to you if you wish or give it to you when you come down. Let me know which you wish me to do. I have been so broken up that I could not write before. Hoping to see you soon I am as every your

Loving Son
W. W. Davis

Saturday, September 15
U.S. Weather Bureau Report
Few strato-cumulus clouds in afternoon and evening. Fresh westerly winds. I. M. Cline, Local Forecast Official still unable to report for duty.

Sunday, September 16
U.S. Weather Bureau Report
Few cumulus and strato-cumulus clouds. Light to fresh westerly winds prevailed. I. M. Cline, Local Forecast Official still unable for duty.

ALICE BLOCK

Alice Block was born in California on January 22, 1881, to Maurice and Rosa Block. Her father arrived in America from Bohemia, now the Czech Republic, in 1867, and her mother emigrated from Germany in 1875. The family moved to Galveston in 1891. She received her teaching degree from Sam Houston State Teachers College and returned to Galveston to begin her career. At the time of the storm, she and her older brother, Sig, lived with their parents at 1911 Twenty-first Street.

After the storm, Miss Alice, as she was affectionately known, taught math and English in the Galveston schools for forty-two years. She remained active in the Temple B'nai Israel and other civic organizations throughout her life. She passed away on February 23, 1977, at the age of ninety-six.

She wrote the following letter to a friend, Jennie Robinson, in Roseland, Texas.

I have been thinking of you and wondering why I had not heard from you. Excuse mistakes as I am still rather stiff and nervous.

SEPTEMBER 16

My dear Jennie;

Your letter of 3rd received. Why, I have been in Galveston ever since school closed.

Dear Jennie, within this past week I have passed through the most trying experience of my life; You have no idea of the havoc, distress and desolation that can be caused by wind and water. Of course you have heard of the terrible storm that reached us here on the 8th. I shall tell you of my own personal experience.

We were living in a two storied house not quite two blocks from the beach. About ten o'clock Saturday morning the overflow began and by five o'clock the water in the house was so high that it was impossible to remain downstairs; the wind was terrific and the water was rapidly rising. I watched all the houses south of us go down one after another, and then felt that our time was coming next. I tried to prepare my dear old parents for the ordeal.

A little after six our house fell down on its side. We got on the bed, and I opened a window above our heads, and held open the blinds, for my parents to get out and then followed. We were then wedged in a triangular place scarcely able to keep our heads above the water. I then

19. Twenty-first Street and Avenue P½. "We were living in a two storied house not quite two blocks from the beach."—Alice Block

saw a flat roof floating above my head and climbed on there; when I found it safe, my parents followed me.

In the meantime the mud had torn nearly all my clothes from me. Just as we all got on the roof, our house went down in pieces and we have never seen any more of it nor any of our possessions since.

Thus in the beating rain, all most naked, with timber and other things being hurled around us by the wind we drifted five or six hours. Constantly we were struck by flying missiles. At one time my mother was struck in the head, and a gash cut. My father was struck in the chest and for a few moments was unconscious, and had I not held him up, would have drowned. After drifting for so long we finally saw a house for which we swam, the house was a total wreck, but still, as the water began to fall it protected us from the rain, though not the wind; and we were so cold, oh so cold.

About 7 o'clock Sunday morning we received some assistance. Mamma and Papa have both been unwell since then, Mamma for a few days being very sick. It was surely through God's mercy that I kept my presence of mind all that terrible night and brought my parents through alive. Although all I have in this world that I can call my own, is a shirt waist and a skirt, I still feel thankful that we are all alive.

I intended to substitute in the Galveston schools this session, but all the school buildings are badly damaged and it is impossible to tell when school will begin.[38] I shall work in a store for a few days and I must work at something as it is absolutely necessary for me to do something in our present destitute condition. Write me a long letter at once. With love,

Your friend
Alice Block

Monday, September 17
U.S. Weather Bureau Report
Few cumulus, strato-cumulus and alto-stratus clouds. Light to fresh westerly winds becoming southerly. I. M. Cline, Local Forecast Official, returned for duty this afternoon. Mr. Guy C. Harris was employed as a temporary printer today in accordance with telegraph dated September the 15th, 1900.

Mr. Earnest E. Kuhnel, Map Distributor, deserted station and has not been seen since 5 p.m. Saturday. I have been informed that he left

20. Bath Avenue school, located on Twenty-fifth Street and Avenue P, only a few blocks from Alice Block's home. "I intended to substitute in the Galveston schools this session, but all the school buildings are badly damaged."—Alice Block

Galveston this morning without letting anyone in office know anything about it. Thunderstorm in early morning; time of beginning and ending unknown.

ELEANOR HERTFORD

Eleanor "Nell" Hertford lived with her sister, Louise Hertford Beadles, and brother-in-law, Walter "Bess" Beadles at 1503 Broadway. Walter Beadles, a good friend of the Gonzales family, was involved in the cotton business. The letter was addressed to artist Boyer Gonzales, who missed the storm because he was painting in Prouts Neck, Maine, with Winslow Homer. Boyer's brother, Julian "Alcie" Gonzales occupied the Gonzales home at 3327 Avenue O during the storm.

Eleanor Hertford became Mrs. Boyer Gonzales in 1907.

My dear Mr. Gonzales

Bess has just handed me your letter and we all appreciate it so much. How thankful you should be that you were so many miles away from here on that memorable 8th day of September. It would be impossible for any one to describe the horrors of the whole thing as they really were. To read the papers telling of it is like hearing children's prattle in comparison to the reality. I guess those away from here, who have been in suspense have really suffered more than the ones who were here to experience it *all,* for every one here seems *stunned,* and you never see any emotion displayed of any kind. Every one is perfectly calm! We all seem to have gone through so much, that we seem beyond tears!

At noon, when I saw people being brought in from the beach, I became very much frightened and excited and begged them all to leave this house and go to Mrs. Gresham's as the wind was coming from the north east and this house was rocking so terribly, but Mamma and Bess wouldn't listen to me.[39] The Bowens have been renting the Campbell house for the summer, so about 5 p.m. Mr. B- came over and told us we were in danger as part of the roof was gone.[40] We went out into the water which was to our waists, but couldn't go against the wind then to Mrs. Gresham's, so thinking of course that the Campbell house was safer than ours, we went there.

That same calm which is prevailing over the whole town took possession of me then and I was able to be of great assistance to the men in keeping the door from coming in. The whole roof came in on us, and 16 of us were huddled in the vestibule. I think we could not have stood it a half an hour longer, for when the front doors gave way we knew we should only go out to be drowned, as 'twas moonlight and we could see how high the water was.

We fully realized our danger and stayed as closely together as possible, so if we perished we would all four go. After the water receded we went to Mrs. Lobit, which was damaged very slightly, and there we stayed for two nights, as this house is not habitable when it rains.[41] But Mr. Gonzales, I had so fully made up my mind that we were going to die that night that 'twas the longest time before I could fully realize that the storm was over and we all safe!

But the whole town is a perfect *wreck,* you can't picture the *awfulness* of it all, and as for dead bodies, we couldn't sit on the galleries at all without seeing wagon loads of them going by. At first, people didn't realize there would be so many, and they were carried by one at a time on litters, but later they had to be carted away like so much debris. There were two wagons full taken from the wreck right here in front of us on the esplanade and the poor things had stiffened in the positions in which they died, most of them with their hands clasped high in the air, in the attitude of prayer.[42] The ones I saw will haunt me to my dying day!

21. "There were two wagons full taken from the wreck right here in front of us."
—Eleanor Hertford

22. Photo sent to Boyer Gonzales showing his brother Alcie Gonzales in front of the family home. "Alcie came to hunt us up the day after the storm."—Eleanor Hertford

Louise and I are begging Bess to go away from here to live, I would gladly turn my back on Galveston forever! But of course we have no plans made as yet. Alcie came to hunt us up the day after the storm, and drops in every once in a while to cheer us all, although he is one of the busiest men in town. He said he would probably come here and stay until your house could be fixed. He is now staying with Mrs. Brown.[43]

Well, I think I had better wind up this gruesome letter, and I only wish I could have written a more cheerful account. We have all been sick. I think from the terrible odor, and living on canned goods and brackish water, but we are all right now. If I was selfish I would wish you were here to make us all feel better, but for your own sake I advise you not to come home if you can possibly help it. We all send our love to you and hope you will write often.

Nell.

JOSEPH HENRY HAWLEY

J. H. (Joseph Henry) Hawley, a railroad executive, played an instrumental role during the city's organization for recovery after the storm as chairman of the Committee of Public Safety.

He recounts his experiences and activities to his estranged second wife (Julia Raine Hawley), whom he would later divorce, and his daughter, Mary Hawley Willis (Mrs. Short A.). His brother, Robert Bradley Hawley, was the Republican U.S. Representative from Galveston. Mr. Hawley refers to his son, Harry Hawley, and his wife, Sarah, and then infant Harry, Jr. Sarah's letter to her parents appeared earlier.

SEPTEMBER 18

My dear wife and daughter:-

This is the first time in the rush of business and other duties which have fallen to my lot, in which I could calmly sit down and write you of the events which have transpired since Sep't 8th. Our office desks and furniture of every description, papers etc., are a total wreck and I have had so many thousand things to do and so many people to talk to that I could not do more than wire you from time to time. Do not think it strange of me that I have not written but I have not had a typewriter in the office and the time required for such a letter as I feel the occasion demanded, could not be spared.

I have sent you the copies of the *Daily News* and the *Houston Post* daily and have arranged with the *Galveston News* to send you a copy of the paper for a month, that you may keep posted as to current events. It is evident from your telegrams to me that the mere statement that I was safe and well was not sufficient and I will therefore endeavor to give you some details that will be of some interest.

I was apprised very early on the day of the 8th, of the likelihood of the great storm which swept over the city, beginning about 3 o'clock and ending at 12 o'clock at night, and took early precautions to protect the property at home and such other property under my charge, as far as practicable. I had, of course, no idea of the extent to which it would go. Water in this office was four feet high, in fact over all the counters, overthrowing all the desks and other furniture, mixing it up in an inextricable mass of confusion.[44] The wharf front from one end of it to the other is a mass of wreckage and sunken vessels. Business houses were crushed, carrying down valuable goods and in many cases valuable lives. Fully 5,000 people lost their lives and fully 3,000 more suffer from injuries from slight to serious wounds.

The whole territory from 9th St., east, out to the beach, and then for a distance of four and one half blocks of the densely populated district, clear out to Woollam's Lake and beyond the Harris' house, has been swept away and fully two thirds of the inhabitants given up to the angry waves.[45]

It is impossible at this time to enumerate single instances but I cannot refrain from mentioning Mrs. Wakelee, whom you no doubt remember.[46] Early on Monday morning when going through the long row of bodies in the morgue, I lifted the pall, and found beneath it, with a faint smile on her lips, Mrs. Wakelee, with her gray hair all matted and streaming in disordered confusion about her shoulders.

I next lifted up the pall of Walter Fisher, the husband of Lillie Harris,

23. "I superintended the handling of 500 bodies over the wharves at Galveston on to barges."—Joseph H. Hawley

and then came to Richard Swain, who no doubt you remember, but these are simply nothing compared to the great mass of people who lost their lives.[47] I superintended the handling of 500 bodies over the wharves at Galveston on to barges, whence they were taken out to sea, with weights attached to them and sunk, as the only means, at that time, by which they could be disposed of; at different points along the wreckage funeral pyres were erected and 10, 12, 14 to 16 bodies piled thereon, saturated with oil and burned, while hundreds of bodies were burned in individual instances. On Monday it was ascertained it was utterly impossible to dispose otherwise of the bodies except by giving them up to the sea or by cremation.

Lillie Harris Fisher and all her children are dead; also Miss Rebecca Harris and three of the Davenport children—but one of the Davenport children being saved.[48] Davenport, with a voice steady with the strength of a man, told me all the details, and simply laid his hand in mine and said, "Mr. Hawley, we know you mourn with us. I am grateful to God for the saving of our little daughter."

Every man here has nerve and has tried to do his duty—the measure of it was that which he could do. For two days and two nights we stayed up, not knowing even that we were tired, until we could go no further. Instances of courage and heroism are thick, for every man seemed to have the courage necessary to meet such an occasion.

Harry and Sarah and the baby, passed a most dreadful night with flying timbers etc., bombarding the house in which they were, but they survived, and while they were at my house looking for me, I was at their house looking for them, and the baby, when I got there, was sleeping peacefully, although, as the servants said,—he was hungry. Harry and Sarah went on board the *SS "MEXICAN"* on Wednesday evening and remained there until Friday, when the ship left here for New Orleans, from which point Harry, Sarah and the baby will take train for Litchfield. It is Harry's intention, as soon as he has arranged for Sarah and the baby, to return at once to his duties in Galveston. It will be a great disappointment if he fails to do so. Mr. McVitie expressed himself to me yesterday, as being very tenderly attached to Harry, but was afraid he would not return, on account of the expressed fears he had of the situation here.[49]

The storm has left the city without drainage and the limited supply of water prevents us from giving much attention, at present, to our sanitary condition. The wreckage I have referred to is fully 100 feet deep and in many places 25 feet high, undoubtedly underneath which, there still re-

24. Funeral barge being towed out to sea

mains a great number of bodies yet to be found. Of course you understand the accumulation of filth etc., the stench, arising from the lack of drainage of perhaps 40,000 people, must produce sanitary conditions injurious to the health in the last degree.

The weather is intensely hot, since the 8th of Sep't to the present time. The weather has been perfectly clear and with the sun beating down on it, odors arise making it most unbearable. There is no place today in our country that is not a more desirable locality than Galveston, for the weak and helpless. I cannot invoke too strongly your remaining away from Galveston for a time, until we have gotten the city into a condition to receive healthy people. We will do all that human hands can do. 2,000 men are employed daily cleaning up, but this will not be accomplished in less than four or five weeks of constant work. We are gradually coming up out of the disaster which settled over the city, and we know that with

25. "The wreckage I have referred to is fully 100 feet deep and in many places 25 feet high."—Joseph H. Hawley

our locality, deep water and our commercial importance, that we will build a city here along modern lines, which will attract citizenship from all parts of the world.

Bradley is here, working hard with his full faculties, encouraging and doing great work and good, as everybody has abiding confidence in him.[50] I showed him your letter, in which you refer to his consideration and I must confess it seems wonderful that he should have thought of the matter in the way that he did. It simply relieved me beyond expression, for when he arrived here he rushed into my arms in one long embrace. I never felt he had the true and abiding affection which he has exhibited. He tells me to send you his sincerest and truest love and hopes to meet you all very soon.

His house did not suffer any more than ours. The house on [Avenue] H has the weather vane bent also the dining room chimney blown down. It fell on the gallery roof, crushing a hole through same, through which the rain poured onto the gallery. The east side of the house was bombarded with bricks. There is a small leak in my room, knocking down about 12 inches square of plastering. Outside of some other small things the house is uninjured. The yard is filled with all kinds of stuff,—paving blocks etc., but there is no serious damage to the property otherwise. $200.00 will cover all loss and I am rapidly putting the place into shape.

I had the entire roof gone over about two weeks ago and fastened down with new nails—scraped and repainted by a contractor S. G. Cornett, who was recommended to me by Mr. Willie R. Johnson, so that we did not lose any part of the top hamper of the house, except the injuries I have referred to.[51] We lost the side and back fences and the cistern floated over to another part of the yard but was wholly uninjured, only requiring setting up again. All of this is now being done and the premises will be in order in the course of the next two weeks. The rooms of course where the paper came down will have to be plastered at the points designated and the rooms repapered, but that will be a nominal expense. The iron fence in front of the property is still in position, although a great deal of wreck-

26. "2000 men are employed daily cleaning up."—Joseph H. Hawley

age—telegraph poles, paving blocks etc. has lodged against it, is it yet undamaged, it resisting all attacks.

By scanning the lists published in the papers you will be able to gather items of persons whose lives were lost. There were a great many narrow escapes of friends of yours. J. M. Brown's residence was spared.[52] All the glass in the east side of the Willis' residence was blown out, and many of the beautiful wall frescoes, put in at heavy cost were ruined.[53] Frank Walthew made his house a place of refuge for all persons during the storm. The Willis House on Broadway and Tremont is still standing. As I passed there early Sunday morning, wading in the water, Stella called to me from one of the upper windows and told me she was all right and we metaphorically shook hands over the fact. Her father did not reach Galveston for several days and it took me a considerable time, after he reached here, to convince him that all were safe, as he was on the mainland and entirely without communication.

I have not heard a word from Mr. and Mrs. Haygood, who were at Alvin. I have not however seen their names in the lists of the lost. E. D. Cavin and his family were saved, although they were almost in the deepest part of the flood.[54] The Porters were all saved, as likewise were Dr. Fisher and his family.[55]

One of the saddest deaths was that of Stanley G. Spencer.[56] He was compelled by the rising waters to seek refuge up to[w]n and was unable to reach his home. I saw Mrs. Spencer two days afterwards, and hearing about the body of S. G. Spencer being in the ruins and being brought to the morgue we found his face unmarked by violence although the back part of his head was crushed in. She bears her misfortune bravely. E. E. Rice's family were saved.[57] Daisy L. Davis and her cherub, also Waters was saved, although Waters was forced to stay in the Cotton Mills all night, up to his neck in water.[58]

I will not prolong this letter now. It is with the deepest gratitude we can say that all of our immediate family were saved and sound, and that the loss which has been sustained in each case is as near nominal as such a great disaster could possibly permit. Money and contributions of clothes is coming to us from every quarter. I am advised today of one check, coming from one firm, being $50,000.00 in amount. The whole world seems to have arisen in sympathy and help is coming from Paris, Bremen, Liverpool, London, Hamburg, as well as provisions, nurses, physicians, and other offerings are coming from every portion and part of the country. We will have rail connection over the bridge, not later than Friday next, at least and we will then be in communication with the outside world, in a business way.

Give my love to all, and believe me ever and always your

Husband and father.
J. H. Hawley
[signed]

Mrs. Masterson was lost, Lucian Minor and all but three houses in Denver Resurvey were lost.[59] Miss Bettie Brown waved her handkerchief to me as I passed their house the morning after the storm and has since driven over the city as far as practicable.[60]

I send the copy of this letter to your mother. Will write you very often now short but pointed letters.

Your affectionate
Father.

JAMES BROWN

James Brown and his wife, Sarah ("Sallie"), emigrated from England in 1883 with their two daughters, Grace and Winnifred. In 1900 they moved to Galveston from Flatonia, Texas, and Mr. Brown worked for an unidentified dairy west of the city. His wife and now-married daughters stayed in the house at the southwest corner of 21st and Avenue L.

OCTOBER 7

Dear Sisters and Cousins,

I am writing this to you all, for I suppose you will perhaps forward it to them. We are all well and alive thank God! You will no doubt have read about the awful flood that has devastated this City and swept thousands into Eternity. We were all living here, myself, Sallie, Winnie, her husband and three children, Gracie and her husband. Winnie and her family had only been a day or two here, they were all living in one house with Sallie. I would like to describe the awful tornado and flood but words cannot describe it,—perhaps you have read accounts of it and seen pictures of the wrecks, but if you put them all together and multiply the awfulness of it by ten, you will have but a faint idea of it all. Human thought cannot grasp it.

As you are aware it occurred on Saturday the 8th of Sept. Nothing previous to denote any storm coming only the usual warning from the signal station which no one notices. I was managing a dairy for a gentleman in the City, and live in the house about 1½ miles from my people and was up early in the morning, about two o'clock. At that time I noticed a deal of water in the streets, up to the horses' belly but paid no more attention to it,—but as morning came and the wind increased and blowing hard directly opposite to the Gulf waves and so kept them back, but piled them away in the Gulf here, then this island, the water continued to rise through the day and by three o'clock became very dangerous, about 5 feet deep in our yard.

We, that is the family I was with, stood on our front gallery, the house being elevated about five or six feet above the ground, and saw house after house float in the Gulf, and men, women, and children coming to our house for protection, in all about 20 people. The water still rose and began coming in our house, then the wind came right in the Gulf, and blew a hurricane and brought the waves in fast and furious; windows began to smash and the house began to creak, and we men propped the front of the house with planks, the woman and children standing on tables. It was then dark and the Mistress of the house said to me, "Mr. Brown don't leave us" (the Master not being home—was at his business in the City and it was impossible for him to get home we being within a hundred yards of the Gulf got the full force of the wind and waves).

At that time a tremendous tidal wave came and smashed the whole front of the house in and filled it with water, then there was screaming of the people. I got hold of the mistress by the arm and got her into another room trying to get out at the back but coming to the next door there was some wreckage and I had to leave hold of her to push it away and I could not find her anymore, although I felt all I could for her. I then swam through a kitchen which was latticed round, and climbed outside and got upon some drift wood that had lodged there and a boy joined me on it. We then saw the house collapse and half of it was coming over us.

I said to the boy, "John we are surely gone", but I ran along the raft from the house and I saw a small twig . . . and caught hold of it and found it was fast. I then got hold of some more and then felt a branch with my feet. The boy followed me and he got hold with help, he was nearly scared to death and prayed and cried. I told him to hang on for dear life and not get scared. The waves were sometimes six feet above our heads and we only got breath occasionally. At one time we thought we had gone, for a house came floating behind, and I thought it would have gone over us, I don't know where it went to.

We remained in that tree all that night till the water went down. What became of the people in our house? Why all were drowned and the house gone and every house for miles. I was crazy to get home and dreading the worst, for such devastation was wrought on every hand, and after climbing over houses and bodies I came in sight of it and Lo it was standing and all my folks safe and sound and looking for me. Now what was to be done to clear the City; it was put under Martial law and every man was impressed at the point of the bayonet to help clear.

About twenty men were shot dead for robbing the dead of rings and jewelry, life was not worth a penny, they found so many dead they had to haul them by the wagon load and throw them in the Gulf or burn them, anything to get rid of them. But now about food, it was nearly all gone but what there was in the city was given up and distributed and as soon as the outside world heard of the sad affair, they sent provisions by the trainload, and there was no need of anyone going hungry, and clothing in abundance for all. But money is very scarce for it takes so much to clear the streets of debris and clean up and disinfect the City.

I left Flatonia last February and we took a large house here and furnished and rented rooms off, but when the water had gone a great deal of our furniture was spoiled and I lost every bit of my clothes, and when I got off the tree I did not have a shirt nor shoes nor hat nor coat in the world, but there were hundreds worse off than us, for they did not have any shelter and we did. It is very pleasing to us all here to read of the nations of the world responding so liberally to our wants and proves conclusively that "One touch of nature makes the whole world kin." I am wearing clothes now sent from Ohio. I want to get a cow as soon as I can for there is a great demand for milk here at good prices, for nearly the whole of the livestock was drowned. There is everything in the wreckage to get except live stock.

I have been very busy ever since and have had no time to spare or I should have written sooner. I hope you will write soon and tell me how

27. ". . . such devastation was wrought on every hand."—James Brown

you all are as I am anxious to hear. We are all well. Our daughter Gracie and her husband have gone to live in the City of Austin, the Capital of this State.—they got scared of this City.

Sallie joins me in love to all and write soon to us,

Your affectionate brother
Jas. Brown

WINNIFRED CLAMP

Mr. Brown's daughter, Winnifred Clamp, who was visiting with her husband, penned the next account in October, six weeks after the storm. She mentions that she could write in great detail but has lost interest.

OCTOBER 24

Dear Cousin Robt;

Your letter reached me here in Galveston. I will first relieve your fear, and tell you that we are all safe and well. I came on a visit to Mama, a month before the storm, so of course I passed that awful night with them. We are more than lucky to have escaped with our lives. Every moment we expected the house to blow over, and either be crushed in the ruins or drowned. The suspense was simply dreadful.

We were all shut in one room, twelve people counting the children. Grace and I and our husbands, some roomers and Mama. Papa was not there. He passed the night in a tree and on a raft. The house he was working at floated away and all were drowned, except Papa, he managed to get out a transom. We only suffered from our fears and as we went upstairs as soon as the water rose, we were dry, but he was in the water all night. We were delighted when we saw he was saved, and he was overjoyed at seeing us. Such a time!

A good deal of the furniture was ruined, and of course the carpets on the lower floor. Of course I could write many pages about the flood, but I've heard so much and seen so much that I have lost interest. Galveston is building up right along. Grace and her husband went to Austin after the storm and now she has a little boy over a week old. They will return here very soon.

I have three children, one little boy died before I left Bracketh. Mama and Papa will write to you, if not with me, soon. Mama is always talking of coming to England. I too, should be pleased to see you all. Perhaps we may all meet some day, who knows? Of course I don't remember much about England, but what little I do remember is very pleasant. I hope to hear from some of you again. Please give my love to all my relations, and tell Aunt Sarah that Papa is very much alive and hopes to see you all one day. Both join me in love to you all and don't forget to write to,

Your Cousin,
Winnifred B. Clamp

IDA SMITH AUSTIN

Ida Smith Austin, best known for her Bible class at First Presbyterian Church in Galveston, which she founded in 1884, lived with her husband, Valery E. Austin, at 1502 Avenue D. Her brother-in-law, Henry Austin, was the pastor of Broadway Memorial Presbyterian Church, also in Galveston.

Her account appears to be more a memoir than a letter, as it is not addressed to anyone in particular. However, it is included in this section because it was dated just under two months after the storm.

NOVEMBER 6

The story of Galveston's tragedy can never be written. Galveston! the beautiful Island city is hardly recognizable today. A storm had been predicted for Friday night the seventh of September, but so little impression did it make on my mind that a most beautiful and well attended moonlight fete was given at our home Oak Lawn that night.[61] Every one remarked on the beauty of the night. The moon was glorious and there was nothing to indicate that the next evening at that hour many who were there so thoroughly enjoying themselves would be homeless and five at least of that number be where the surges have ceased to roll and the weary are at rest.

I was busy about my domestic affairs Saturday rearranging my house and having chairs, tables, etc., removed from the lawn and was much startled at two o'clock when I heard a man who ran up the street exclaim, "My God! The waters of the bay and gulf have met on Fifteenth Street." I went on the gallery to realize that what he said was only too true. But I felt no uneasiness and remarked to my niece, "We have nothing to fear, the water has never been over our place," and I just felt that it could not come. In a few minutes we heard the lapping of the salt water against the side-walk, and then it slowly crept into the yard.

We began to think it might come into the house so moved all portable furniture, silver, cut-glass, china and bric-a-brac upstairs. In an incredibly short time the water surged over the gallery driven by a furiously blowing wind. Trees began to fall, slate shingles, planks and debris of every imaginable kind were being hurled through the air. We brought our cow on the gallery to save her life but soon had to take her in the dining room where she spent the night. Ten very large trees were soon uprooted and fell crashing, banging, and scraping against our house. We opened all downstairs doors and let the water flow through. Soon it stood three feet in all the rooms.

The wind seemed to grow more furious reaching the incredible velocity of one hundred and twenty miles an hour. Blinds were torn off windows, frames, sash and all blown in, and the rain water stood an inch and a half on upstairs floors. Then slowly dripped through taking paper and plastering from ceilings in rooms below.

As Mr. Austin was not in the city, we, my niece and myself being alone in the house were very uneasy, though we did not feel as if our house

28. Oak Lawn, 1502 Avenue D. Valery Austin Residence

would go to pieces. When the storm was at its height, two gentlemen friends who remembered that we were alone struggled through the water which reached to their necks to render us any assistance possible taking us out of the house if necessary. But soon the water began to recede and it went out as rapidly as it had come in.

The excitement and nervous strain had made us very hungry and one of the gentlemen said he would milk the cow, and together with coffee made on a chafing dish and some cold bread we had a midnight spread. When daylight came and we could see the havoc which had been wrought in other portions of the city, we only felt gratitude to Almighty God that our lives had been spared and ceased to consider our property loss for a minute. One trying feature of the storm was that we had no light except candles. Gas and electricity were both things of the past, as the electric power house and gas works were among the first structures to go down.[62]

Sunday every one seemed dazed and stunned, but looking for and burying the dead were begun in earnest. Three morgues were established but it took a very short time to convince the most hopeful that it would be impossible to place bodies in morgues for identification and that the number who had perished was so great, they would have to be buried at sea, as the quickest way to dispose of them.

Men were impressed to search for the dead, and they were piled on

29. Brush Electric Company powerhouse. ". . . the electric power house and gas works were among the first structures to go down."—Ida Smith Austin

wagons, drays and floats and taken to the wharf, where they were weighted, put upon barges and towed out to sea. The mournful dirges of the breakers which lashed the beach, the sobbing waves and sighing winds, God's great funeral choir, said their sad requiem around the dead.

The sea as though it could never be satisfied with its gruesome work washed these bodies back upon the shore, the waves being the hearses that carried them in to be buried under the sand. The terrible odor from thousands of putrefying bodies was almost unbearable. Soon it was decided the only thing that could be done to save the city from pestilence was to burn the bodies of both animals and people. Wherever they were found, lumber from the wreckage was piled upon them and they were incinerated.

The loss of life will not fall far short of six thousand. The property loss will reach the enormous sum of thirty millions. Over four thousand happy homes absolutely demolished and the wreckage of these homes was piled from twenty to thirty feet high for miles along the gulf front, extending inland from three hundred to a thousand yards. This wreckage formed almost a solid break-water and in order to get through it with teams a road-way was hewn out which was as difficult as cutting a passage through a hill thirty feet high. Most of this debris has been turned over looking for the dead and a great deal of it hauled to vacant lots to clear out the streets.

Many of those who lived in the storm swept district have pitched tents on the very lots where their homes were destroyed. Whole families have been lost. Captain Richard Hope Peek, a graduate of the V.M.I. who will be pleasantly remembered by many Lexingtonians, his wife and six children perished.[63] Their bodies were found several days afterwards all tied together and Captain Peek was identified by his class ring. His home was in Denver Resurvey, a western suburb of the city of which only three houses much damaged remain. Although our connection was largely consisting of five families located in different parts of the city, all survived the storm.

My brother-in-law, Rev. Henry Austin, pastor of Broadway Memorial Presbyterian Church lost his house and his church was badly wrecked, but his family escaped. Being entirely cut off from the mainland for several days, telegraph, telephone, and railway communications being washed

30. Saint Patrick's Catholic Church. "The loss of church property is astounding." *—Ida Smith Austin*

away we were sadly in need of food and a water famine was dreaded. The city water works were demolished and cisterns were filled with salt spray. Fortunately the water works were put in sufficient order to furnish a limited supply of fresh water in a few days.

News of our distressed condition was carried to Houston by means of boats as soon as possible. Everybody seemed as full of sympathy as we were of anguish and manifested it at once by sending food, clothing, and money. There was never a needier call more liberally responded to from America and abroad. It was with personal pleasure I noticed a donation [from] Lexington, my childhood home.

The loss of church property is astounding. Thirty church buildings suffered loss, more than twenty were completely destroyed. Fully six hundred thousand dollars of property and more than fifteen hundred church members would be a conservative estimate. Bodies are still being found after two months, but Galvestonians are a brave people and they are taking heart again and are busy trying to rehabilitate their city and their homes.

The necessity of work for all classes has been the salvation of the city. The hearts of visitors were stirred as they witnessed the enthusiasm with which mere women and even children heroically grappled with the unparalleled situation and out of chaos brought order and in the midst of seeming destruction rose triumphantly to a nobler purpose and unselfish devotion. Galveston will be rebuilt more beautiful, more massive, more enduring than before.

As the oak sinks its roots more deeply and grows more rugged by the storms which seek its destruction so out of this dread experience shall Galveston grow to great strength and greater influence. Gratitude fills my heart that God has spared so many useful lives yet mingled with it is deepest sorrow for those who suffered the loss of all they held dearest and best.

Ida Smith Austin

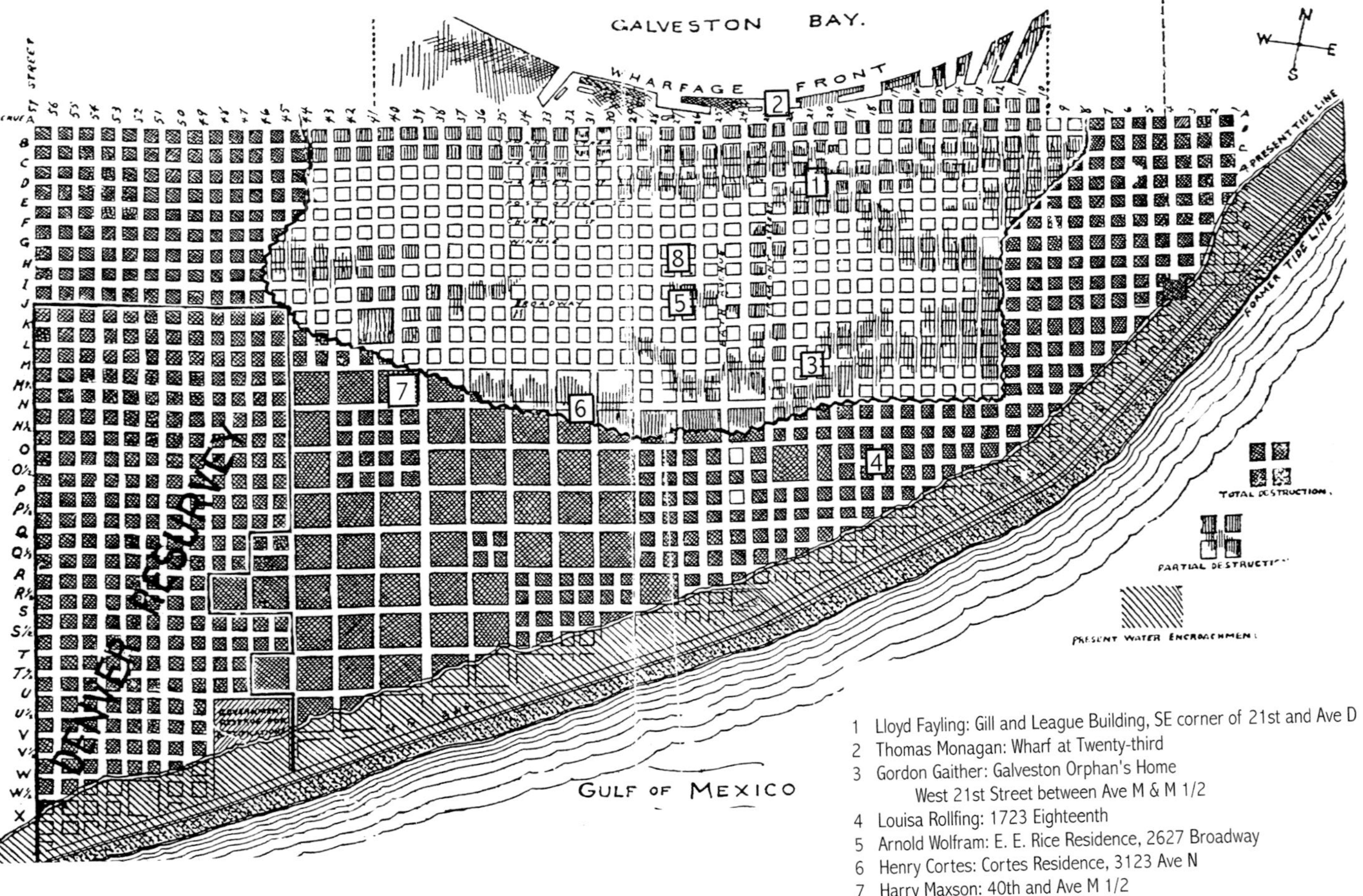

1 Lloyd Fayling: Gill and League Building, SE corner of 21st and Ave D
2 Thomas Monagan: Wharf at Twenty-third
3 Gordon Gaither: Galveston Orphan's Home
West 21st Street between Ave M & M 1/2
4 Louisa Rollfing: 1723 Eighteenth
5 Arnold Wolfram: E. E. Rice Residence, 2627 Broadway
6 Henry Cortes: Cortes Residence, 3123 Ave N
7 Harry Maxson: 40th and Ave M 1/2
8 Geneva Dibrell Scholes: 2709 Ave H

Survivor Memoirs

LLOYD R. D. FAYLING

Lloyd R. D. Fayling came to Galveston in 1900 as district manager for a New England publishing syndicate. Prior to the Spanish-American War, he was stationed in Cuba as a St. Louis newspaper correspondent and returned to Columbus, Ohio, after the war began to raise a company of volunteers. He also had served as a deputy U.S. Marshal in the 1894 Chicago riots.

His strong sense of military duty led him to report for duty to Galveston police chief Ed Ketchum as soon as the storm subsided. Ketchum ordered Fayling to go around the city collecting militiamen and surviving police officers and organize a force to maintain order and protect citizens from looters. He and his men worked for four days with no sleep and little food and drink. All together, Fayling had approximately three hundred men, including sixty police officers, under his command.

After Adjutant General Thomas Scurry arrived and relieved him of his duty, Fayling assisted a group of men bound for Austin to speak with Gov. Joseph Sayers, as far as Houston. There he met Clara Barton, founder of the American Red Cross, and offered to help her get to Galveston. He then traveled north to raise money for Galveston survivors, visiting both Chicago and his hometown of Kalamazoo, Michigan. In October, 1900, he moved to Montreal to manage a leading Canadian newspaper, the Star.

On Saturday, the 8th, it was raining in Galveston, the rain-storm prophesied by the weather bureau. It had been with us all morning, and it was

31. Maj. Lloyd R. D. Fayling

apparently nearly over. The wind was blowing a stiff gale, and knowing that there must be a heavy sea running in the Gulf, at about one o'clock I started for the beach to get a view of the storm.

An acquaintance passing in a buggy gave me a ride to the beach, and we found the water from M street south as deep as the hubs of the buggy. People were already somewhat alarmed at the situation, but no one thought that the storm was going to be anything more than one of our usual damp spells.

My acquaintance left me a block from the beach to bring some ladies into the center of the city, and I waded and swam the rest of the way to the Midway Road to get a good view of the sea. Within a few minutes of my joining the group standing in the wrecked street, O'Keefe's bathing pavilion and half of the Pagoda went down. Murdoch's pavilion was also beginning to break up.[1]

The crowd at the beach knew me very well, as I had been swimming several hours a day there all summer, and they began to chaff me good naturedly about losing that new bathing suit of mine, which was of a particularly vivid color and attracted some attention.

I told them in a bantering way that it had probably gone out to sea, and then one of the Pagoda attendants came along and said that it was still in the building. I suggested that he go and get it, but as he seemed to doubt that he would ever come back, I went there and got it myself.

The Pagoda is a building extending out into the sea on piling, with a long walk supported also by pilings connecting it with the beach. From the Pagoda I got a close view of the sea, closer than I could have got from the beach, and as the waves were wetting me while out there, I noticed their phosphorescent color, as well as the fact that the wind was blowing a gale from the north while the waves were running against the wind instead of with it.

I had seen these same signs in the West Indies while there on military service, and had found that they meant a hurricane. I then realized that something was going to drop, and started for town, bathing suit in hand,

32. "The Pagoda is a building extending out into the sea on piling, with a long walk."—Lloyd R. D. Fayling

and informed all the people I met that they had better get into the higher parts of the town.

By the time I reached the YMCA building the storm struck and several buildings had gone, and masonry, bricks and slate were coming pretty thick. I was wading through an average of five feet of water, and could not make rapid progress, and I was kept busy dodging live wires which were sputtering and burning in a dozen directions.

There were a few ladies at this time on the streets who were evidently trying to make their way home, but several were blown away by the wind, and carried distances of 10 to 20 feet into the water. It was almost impossible at this time to stand against the wind, but I was fortunately able to fish out a few ladies and help them into the YMCA building where they were quite safe.[2]

I got to my office at 21st and Market streets as fast as possible, as my heavy clothing, wet mackintosh and umbrella were a little undesirable for the dampness. I still had my bathing suit in hand, probably the only one left in town, as everyone stored them at the beach. I quickly got into it, put on a pair of stout Turkish slippers, and my rainy-day suit was complete.

There was no one in the Gill and League Building but Dr. Baldinger and Dr. Nave, two physicians, and a young lady named Miss George who had been brought there for safety by Dr. Nave.[3] It was a hungry looking crowd, so I swam across the street to the Four Seasons restaurant, where they were putting all the eatables on the higher shelves.[4] The young man said he could not serve me, as he was afraid to stay much longer for fear he would be drowned.

The water was about five feet deep in the restaurant. I found he had some hot coffee, however, and I told him if he did not get me some supper he would be drowned right then. So he waded around and got me a hearty meal and an armload of provisions for the people across the street. I carried over the provisions, also brought in an old gentleman of about 75 and a young man of 20 who were very nearly drowned and appreciated a dry place.

Things got worse every moment. The wind rocked our place in all directions, and the air seemed to be full of roofs, slate, masonry, telegraph poles and all sorts of things. I brought in a number of people from time to time who came by in the water, which was now running furiously through the streets, the wind having kicked up quite a sea, which was smashing the plate glass windows in the stores.

33. Gill and League Building

Presently a boat came along, a center-board sloop 30 feet long, dismasted and without oars. There were several women and children, and a man in the bow was throwing a coil of rope about posts and telegraph poles endeavoring to stop the boat, which seemed to be headed for the bay.

She came up as rapidly as a steamer, but he managed to check her speed in front of the building, and we caught his rope. At first he did not want to come in, saying that the building had been condemned, but on our assurance that it was one of the safest parts of the city, he thought he had better come upstairs. So we pulled in the boat under the 21st street arched entrance, and made it fast inside the building to the stairway.

He then threw the babies over to me, I threw them to Dr. Baldinger, and Dr. Baldinger to Dr. Nave, and assisted the ladies in a similar way. We soon had them up stairs in a comparatively dry place—that is, we only had two inches of rainwater which had leaked in, as our roof had blown away a few minutes previous, and there was only the flooring above to keep out the rain.

The boat was of considerable use after this, as it enabled us to make short excursions into the street at the end of a rope. A number of people were caught very close to me during the night with bricks and masonry. One poor fellow had his whole face slashed off with a piece of slate only a few feet from me, just as he was within a few steps from the building and safety.

A dozen times bricks and slate missed me by only a few inches, and I only had a narrow margin on several chimneys, but I seemed to be particularly in luck and scarcely got a scratch. My closest personal escape was on one of my excursions to the corner, for I was in and out of the water all night.

I was about 200 feet away from our door when the whole intervening space was filled by a telegraph pole falling with a tangle of wires and some parts of our roof and a lot of stray masonry filled up the space so there was no wading back, and slate seemed to be coming about a million a minute, which obliged me to swim under the water for about a minute, which was very unpleasant as I got tangled up in a number of telegraph wires and thought for a fraction of a second that I would never come up again.

During the night, with the assistance of Dr. Baldinger and Dr. Nave I brought in a total of 43 refugees. Every one of them came through the storm with perfect safety, and were loud in their protestations of gratitude, except about fifteen Negroes and hoboes who spent the night under arrest. These fellows had come in one by one and were straggling up and down the stairway and in the hall and overheard us plan to put the women and children into the boat, cover it with mattresses to keep off the slates, while the men of the party pushed and swam with the craft over to another building.

At that time we expected the building would go every minute as it was shaking back and forth, and this seemed our best way out of the scrape. The Negroes made an attempt to take possession of the boat, but I fortunately had a six-shooter and a Winchester handy, and put them under arrest at pistol point, and stationed my servant, Ed Hearde, the bravest and most faithful Negro that I have ever known, at the door with a Winchester, where he kept guard all night. He also made those Negroes' lives most unhappy ones.

By three o'clock the wind had gone down to merely a strong gale. It seemed like a calm after the night's cyclone, and as everyone in the building decided to stay where they were until morning, and having nothing else to do, I went out on an observation tour and to call on some friends in another part of the city, about whom I felt considerable anxiety.

The water had gone down as rapidly as it rose, and there were not over four or five feet at this time except in spots, so it was comparatively an easy matter to get around, although it cut up my feet pretty badly on tiles and plate glass and wrecked buildings over which one had to climb as high as second story windows.

I found my friends were all safe, as their house was in the higher part of the city, and expecting that I could be of some use down-town, I made my way back. All store windows seemed to be broken, and all sorts of suspicious looking people were crawling over heaps of rubbish and going in and out of stores in the most suspicious manner. It was not yet daylight, but looting had already begun.

As soon as daylight came I hunted up the Chief of Police to turn over my prisoners, but found the city hall partially blown down, and as a police officer told me there was no place left to put any prisoners, I gave them a lecture and a warning all round and turned them loose.

Everything was chaos. It was the worst looking town I ever saw, and I have seen a number of places wrecked by cyclones and other disturbances. There were little knots of people standing on the street corners, frightened out of their wits, while crazy men and women walked up and down the streets crying and weeping at the top of their voices. There were corpses in every direction.

I found the Chief of Police, Ed Ketcham [*sic*], who did not seem to have any policemen left, and asked him if I could be of any service to him. He said most decidedly yes, and found a damp envelope at the Hotel Tremont, upon which he wrote me a commission as Sergeant of Police. His deputy, Gus Amundson also wrote me an authority to supply my men with food and drink and supplies at the expense of the city, same to be used after I had found some men.

I suggested to the city authorities that I had seen several half-naked soldiers wandering around the streets, and told them that in my opinion the only salvation of the town lay in getting it under martial law as quickly as possible. They assured me that they would back me up in every way in anything that I wanted to do, to go right ahead and do what I pleased. But some of them assured me that it was impossible to get any help from the regular soldiers, as they would not obey civilians. Apparently somebody had been trying it.

Within four blocks I found four bare-footed artillery men, and at my command of "Attention" they fell in without any questions, and seemed to be glad to find some sort of an officer. I immediately informed them that they were now policemen, and that I was going to swear them in as soon as I got time, that in the meantime they should fall in and get some shoes, guns, ammunition and provisions. One or two were inclined to ask questions, but not having time to explain just then, I silenced them with the sharp command of "Silence in the ranks."

I saw Captain Ed Rogers on a corner, apparently dressed in his pajamas, and although one would not judge from his appearance at that time, I knew he was a capable and brave man of some military experience. I immediately issued him a verbal commission, and with his assistance, within thirty minutes supplied the men with shoes, guns, clubs and provisions.

I found more soldiers on every corner, and I finally found a militia bugler with his bugle. We immediately blew the Assembly as loudly as possible, which brought us some more recruits from Battery O, and a few stray militiamen. In times of public danger, militiamen always put on their uniforms, I notice, so we began to present quite a martial appearance, thanks principally to the militia.

Within two hours of receiving my commission I had a soldier on guard duty at almost every point of advantage, and went back for more authority. The mayor and chief of police seemed highly satisfied, and as they were very busy with other forms of relief work and forming a committee of public safety, they issued me another commission as Commander in Chief, which read as follows:

> By the authority invested in me as Chairman of the Committee of Public Safety of the City of Galveston, I, J. H. Hawley, do hereby commission L. R. D. Fayling as commander in chief of the military forces and the special deputies police, with the rank of Major only subject to the orders of the undersigned, the Mayor and Chief of Police.
>
> *J. H. Hawley, Chairman Committee of Public Safety*

Major Fayling is hereby authorized to requisition any property that he may require for the use of his forces, and his receipt will be honored by the city of Galveston and any such property be paid for by the city. Approved by order of the Mayor.

Ed Ketchum, Chief of Police.

Col. J. H. Hawley at this time was the chairman of the committee of Public Safety, and by the instructions of the Mayor I obeyed his orders. Col. Hawley was very clear-headed, and handled the situation very well, but I think the greatest credit for prompt action should be given to Mayor Walter C. Jones, who at all times held the situation completely in his grasp, and was by all odds one of the most capable officers under whom I have ever served.

Father Kirwin, a Catholic priest, who should have been a Major General, was acting as aide de camp for the major, and running one or two branches of public service in the most magnificent style.[5] And as all these capable gentlemen were in charge of the work of burying the dead and feeding the living and handling relief matters, I directed my entire attention to obeying orders, and seeing that proper order was maintained at any cost.

We closed the saloons the first morning, meeting some trifling resistance in one or two cases, which a show of arms instantly overcame. My orders to my men were as follows: First: Close all saloons in town. If a man opens up again and sells liquor after being closed, arrest him. Second: Shoot anyone caught looting the dead or desecrating corpses in any way. If anyone resists your authority, shoot. Be very careful not to interfere with good citizens in any way, but investigate all suspicious characters.

These and a few more similar orders were received by me from headquarters, and were strictly obeyed. Within twenty-four hours, finding we needed more men, we called for volunteers, and impressed a few and drafted a few until we had organized the following battalion: Company A, regular U.S. soldiers of Battery O, detailed to me for service by their Captain Rafferty who assured me that he would send me all the soldiers that he had outside the hospital to act under my orders as special policemen.[6]

Captain Rafferty also assured me that he was pleased with the way I was handling the situation, and that he was perfectly willing for his regulars to act under me. I urged Captain Rafferty to take command in my

34. ". . . my personal squad and I patrolled on foot."—Lloyd R. D. Fayling

place as soon as he came in, a day or two after the storm. But the Captain had been injured during the storm, and escaped with only the clothes he stood in, and of course he could not take command without authority from the United States Government. I organized Companies B & C of mixed militia and citizens volunteers, also a troop of cavalry to patrol the outlying districts.

Horses and cattle were straying in every direction in the streets, ownerless, and so anxious for human company that they would run up to every passer-by as if looking for their masters. The horses were glad indeed to come at the order, and it was marvelous to see my cavalrymen making these horses, many of whom had never been under the saddle, climb over great heaps of debris where a man could hardly walk—or rather climb—under ordinary circumstances.

This troop of cavalry always went at full gallop, jumping five and six foot obstructions with horses that had never been taught to jump, and altogether did the most astonishing things that I have ever seen. Of course this was in Texas, where these fellows, right from their cradle are taught to ride.

I wore out two or three horses a day after the second day in patrol duty, as I made it a point to be in every part of the city and to keep moving both day and night, which had a good effect in keeping my sentries awake, they having a superstition among them which I carefully fostered, that I was going to shoot anybody who went to sleep. Of course I would not really have done this, but it was just as well to let them think that I would. I had no cases of sentinels asleep, as I know from personal investigation.

We did not have any horses the first two days; so my personal squad and I patrolled on foot. But two days of those rubbish heaps, which cut up three pairs of shoes for me in two days, left our feet almost in ribbons, so that a cavalry troop was necessary. I have never see such a mixed body of men keep such perfect discipline, and they were altogether the finest lot of fellows that I have ever commanded.

There was not a case of insubordination, although the situation was such that I was forced to use very strict discipline, and sometimes almost harsh methods, but the esprit de corps was splendid, and they worked as long as they had the strength to walk on their feet.

Every day in the armory these brave fellows had to bathe their feet in cold water to enable them to get them into their shoes, and they actually walked miles when they should have been in the hospital. And I never heard a word of complaint. Some of the best men of the city, business and professional, were in the ranks, and they worked as hard as anyone. But by all odds the city has to thank those brave soldiers of Battery O, as nothing could have been done without them.

I did not get any sleep personally until I was relieved from duty by General Scurry, and had, in fact eaten no meals except an occasional sandwich and a cup of coffee taken in the saddle.[7] But we had the city under complete control from the first. Order was absolutely maintained.

We drove hundreds of Negroes at the bayonet point to assist in the work of burning and loading the dead on barges for sea burial, and on one occasion by orders of the Mayor, brought to me by Father Kirwin, we marched to the foot of Tremont street, taking every able-bodied man, white or black, met with, and forced them at the bayonet point to assist in the awful work.

These poor fellows were only kept up on whiskey, which was given to them by the goblet full, but I did not see any drunken men among them. The stench was terrible, and the work was so disgusting that almost every moment these men were forced to stand aside a few moments, their

35. Brig. Gen. Thomas Scurry, adjutant general of Texas

stomachs rebelling at the terrible task. Men would say, "For heavens sake don't make me do that! I won't go, you can shoot me if you want, but I will not and I can not." Our only answer was "Load with ball cartridge, take aim—" and fortunately we never had to go any further. They always threw up their hands and went to work. I do not know whether I would have shot them or not. But of course, as the orders were to do so, I think I would.

I started out on several occasions with a guard of 20 or 30 men, but we found so many exposed places where they were needed that by the time we had got two or three miles off the beach I would not have a man left, and yet I think some of the most successful and efficient work that I did was just at those times, usually 3 or 4 o'clock in the morning, just before day break.

The sentinels never knew just when I would come climbing over the rubbish piles to see if they were awake, and I used to bring a number of strings of prisoners that I reached by thus quietly taking a walk myself, that would have been frightened away by the noise of the approach of a large guard.

As I had two six-shooters and a sabre, we had no trouble in making arrests, even of considerable number of armed Negroes. I took a pistol away personally from a Negro boy six years old. Negro women had large carving knives whetted to the keenest edge; also the men. Nearly everyone in town was armed in some way or other, with or without permission.[8] A large number of arms had been stolen from the gun stores, which caused the Mayor to issue the following proclamation:

> TO THE PUBLIC: September 11, 1900. The city of Galveston being under martial law, and all good citizens being now enrolled in some branch of the Public service, it becomes necessary to preserve the public peace that all arms in this city be placed in the hands of the military. All good citizens forbidden to carry arms except by written permission from the Mayor, Chief of Police or Major Commanding. All good citizens are hereby commanded to deliver all arms and ammunition in the city, and take Major Fayling's receipt.
>
> *Walter C. Jones, Mayor.*

It was under this commission that the men under me, and brought under orders of Col. Hawley, Chairman of the Committee of Public Safety, requisitioned arms and ammunition, shot guns, rifles, etc., from the stores, pistols from the pawn shops, and the said arms and ammunition and uniforms of the armory. When the chief of police relieved the men of my force from duty, as I had sincerely requested upon the arrival of Gen. Scurry, he issued the following receipt:

> Galveston, Sept. 12, 1900
>
> I hereby certify that Major L. R. D. Fayling has turned over to the city authorities all guns, arms, horses, saddles and supplies requisitioned by him or his men according to the orders of the authorities there made during the past week. I receipt hereby for same.
>
> *Ed. Ketcham,*
> *Chief of Police.*

The chief of police informed me that the city was kept in such perfect order by us that such a large force would no longer be necessary, and ordered me to reduce my force to one hundred men. He then suspended this order indefinitely, and gave me positive orders to bring in all my guards from all parts of the city. Although this did not agree in all respect with my own judgment of the situation, I promptly obeyed, and hearing that General Scurry was in town to take command on behalf of the State, I brought in all troops to the Armory as soon as possible, and assembled them there under arms, by order of the chief of police.

He then ordered an inspection drill down at the Hotel Tremont. The men made a fine appearance as they marched down in perfect military order, which was astonishing for such raw recruits, and I formed them in hollow square in front of the hotel. The chief of police kept us waiting for a long time, and he informed me that Gen. Scurry wished to see me personally. I accordingly tendered a report of General Scurry, which was the correct military procedure on my part, but was intercepted by the chief of police, who gave me positive orders not to report to General Scurry or to see General Scurry at that time, but to go back and put my men through the proper form of inspection. I saluted and obeyed without question.

The men had not had any supper and it was now nearly midnight, and as most of them had no dinner they did not feel in very good humor. There were a few citizen volunteers who, not understanding military discipline began to cheer me very loudly, and make such remarks as "We won't work for anybody but the Major. We won't serve under the Chief of Police. What's the matter with the Major? He's all right!"

This made some disturbance in the ranks, and I addressed the men as I had addressed them at the armory before, telling them most emphatically that they were soldiers and that it was their duty to obey as I was doing, blindly and implicitly. I told them that if their orders were to stand on their heads, that I would have that battalion upside down in five minutes. I told them that if they were guilty of any breach of discipline or resented any orders given by the Chief of Police, Mayor or any other authority over them, that, although they were my own men that I would empty my revolvers into the first company that was so guilty of insubordination.

This talk quieted them, and they were in good shape when the Chief of Police appeared to review them a few minutes later. The Chief of Police gave a number of commands from the Manual, which, being those in use at the time of the Civil War, were not recognized by the men, which threw them into some confusion.

During this time, of course, I had nothing to say, but remained at attention. However, during this slight confusion in the ranks, some of the new citizen recruits, for some reason that I could not understand, hissed as the chief of Police walked down the lines, although I immediately suppressed such lax discipline. The chief of police seemed completely able to cope with the situation, as throughout the whole time at Galveston he displayed perfect self-possession and courage. I think he is a very brave man.

The chief of policemen made the men ground arms, told those that owned their own arms that they could take them with them home, and told me personally that I could report to General Scurry. I had already fallen from the saddle that day from sheer faintness and lack of food and sleep, so I made application as follows to General Scurry for twenty-four hours' rest:

> To the Adjutant-General of the City of Galveston, Texas:
> Sir: Having been on active service without sleep or food since last Saturday, the 8th inst., I beg to be relieved of my present commission from the city authorities as Major of the City Volunteers until I can rest and become fit for more duty in the work of relief. After twenty-four hours' rest I beg to tender my services in any capacity whatever to do any kind of duty that may be of use. I am,
>
> *Very respectfully yours,*
> *L. R. D. Fayling*
> *Maj. City Forces.*

By all military precedence the word "Approved" is all that the commanding officer puts upon such an application, but General Scurry very kindly broke the precedent, and instead of the more formal "Approved", endorsed as follows:

> "Your services have been most worthy. I cheerfully relieve you from duty. Thos. Scurry, Adj. Gen."

General Scurry also apologized for the action of the chief of police. He also expressed the same sentiments to Captain Ed. Rogers, my second in command, Adj. Breckenridge, Lieut. McLane and others of my officers. I assured General Scurry, however, that I was not aggrieved at all in the matter, and had no fault to find with any orders that had been given me by my superiors that I was there to obey orders, had done so so far and was ready to keep on as soon as I could get a little sleep.

As soon as this was done I received an invitation to supper from Mr. John Sealy, who had been very kind throughout the whole matter and had given me personal endorsement and support, which I had much appreciated. Mr. Sealy is by all odds the wealthiest man in the South, as well as one of the most popular men in Galveston.[9] I understand that he had given a hundred thousand dollars that day to the relief fund, though we had canned peaches, crackers and ice-water for supper, which illustrates the limited cuisine prevailing at this time in Galveston.

Mr. Sealy assured me personally of his satisfaction with the work the men and myself had done, and testified to their prompt assistance, and a dozen of other prominent citizens told me the same thing on every street corner that night. The city was left without guards, I understand, that night, and I heard some complaints of disorder and looting, but I cannot say anything about this as to my personal knowledge, as I was busy taking my first night's sleep since before the storm.

My next duty was the escorting of a committee of three or four of our most prominent citizens to Houston, which I did, they being sent to the Governor, at the Governor's request, to bring back a large sum of money for the relief work. I found them down at the wharf, stalled in a crowd of about a thousand people, the steamer Lawrence aground at the opposite side, and it looked as though they would get away about week after next. I was fortunately able to procure a boat and took them across to Houston and through the guard lines. Col. Springer, the chairman of the committee, returned soon after with $50,000 in cash, which would have been delayed some days if we had not managed to make very prompt connection for them by Galveston and Texas City.

I was just returning to Galveston, having had officers' transportation issued to me good for any point in the state, when I received a telegram instructing me to meet Miss Clara Barton and her party of eleven, and give them any assistance if I could do so. I also received the following letter from the Mayor of Houston, A. R. Rosenthal, secretary.

Houston, Tex. Sept 15, 1900.
Major L.R.D. Fayling,
Galveston, Tex.

Sir:

We will urgently ask you to represent us in arranging the details of receiving Miss Clara Barton and her party, providing them with information as to the situation in Galveston. We judge your information to be superior to ours, as you and your men have been patrolling every part of the wrecked city. Confident that you will grant this favor, we are,

Very truly yours,
S. H. Brashear, Mayor.
By A. R. Rosenthal, Secretary.

This was pretty short notice, and I had expected to get back to Galveston for more military service, as I was officially yet absent for rest. But I thought I had better help Miss Barton get over there with this relief train and do the resting some other time, so I hustled around and borrowed a corporal's guard of soldiers, induced the proprietor of the Hutchins House to throw a few drummers out of their rooms on the parlor floor, and to reserve the best part of the house for Miss Barton.[10] The drummers were very indignant, and swore in eighteen languages, mostly Hebrew.[11]

However, in fifteen minutes we had quarters arranged which were very fair, as everybody in the town were sleeping in cots at the hotels and such a thing as a room was impossible to obtain in Houston. When Miss Barton's train got in the guards were ready, soldiers at present arms, everything in very martial style, in fact it was the only spice of the theatrical that there was in the whole business.

There was not the slightest hitch in the whole arrangement, and Miss Barton expressed to me personally how very well pleased she was with her reception. She contrasted the reception at Houston with her reception at the Johnstown flood, wherein she explained to the wife of the proprietor of the hotel, they set her down half a mile or so from the station, and she had to walk in through the wet.[12]

She requested me to act as her military aide, although she had General Sears from Washington acting as her private secretary, and I very cheerfully accepted and gave her all the information in my power in regard to the actual conditions. Miss Barton said that she had not come to inspect the work of others or remain in Houston, but wanted to get into Galveston and do whatever she could that would be most useful.[13]

In the morning, a large number of citizens, mostly ladies of Houston, filed up the staircase, and about twenty of them were presented to Miss Barton. I was assured by a fleshy Hebrew gentleman that he was the mayor pro-tem, and accordingly took charge of the whole thing as far as the city of Houston was concerned, and kindly relieved me of all transportation responsibilities.[14] That was very fortunate, as otherwise I should have felt responsible for the fact that Miss Clara Barton spent that night in Texas City in a day coach, which was a very serious thing for a lady of her age and delicate constitution.

But as I had been told by the Hebrew gentleman, commander in chief and mayor pro-tem, that he would arrange everything and attend to everything, and as I only went along as a member of the Barton party, I was in no way responsible.

At Texas City, through somebody's blunder, I don't know whose, there was no boat to meet Miss Barton, and that lady spent the night in a day coach. There was only one possibility of getting her across the bay, and at her urgent request and at that of General Sears, I managed to get across myself before midnight in a sail boat.

I traversed the wharves on foot for about two miles up and down the city trying to get some kind of a boat to get her across that night, and actually found a boat that might have been used, but coming up I was stopped by a militia captain who had just arrived from somewhere up the state, who told me that he did not care if Mrs. McKinley herself was on the other side, he was going to use that boat for guard duty, and was very anxious to put me under arrest personally, only my papers, passes, and commissions were in perfect order.[15] We should have got her across. But as it was, I reported it to the guard on duty who did not care to wake General Scurry, so it was impossible to get her across until the next morning.

Mayor Jones ordered me to report at the Hotel Tremont when martial law was declared, and on my arrival, in the presence of a few prominent citizens, presented me with the following official document.

> Mayor's Office. Walter C. Jones, Mayor. Galveston, Tex. Sept. 22, 1900. —The Mayor of Galveston, in behalf of the citizens of Galveston and in his own behalf, desires to say that the work Major L. R. D. Fayling did for

> the city of Galveston was most magnificent and cannot be expressed in words. He built the foundation upon which a lot of good work has been done. The initiative, courage and discipline displayed by Major Fayling deserve the highest praise. He has the official and personal thanks of the Mayor and citizens.
>
> *Walter C. Jones, Mayor of Galveston*

> Major Fayling: I consider your work was the saving of the city. I thank you personally for your services and loyalty.
>
> *Walter C. Jones, Mayor.*

I was not expecting any bouquets of the sort, but certainly appreciate very much the kind words of the citizens of Galveston, and I appreciate even more the kind things the people in the streets said every day I walked a block or two down town. I was very glad indeed to see martial law replaced by Mayor Jones' personal government, for Mayor Jones had from the beginning handled the situation in a way that no other municipality has ever been able to do.[16] General Scurry did not take charge for the state of Texas, or as Adjutant General of the State, but by proclamation from the Mayor, as Brigadier General Thos. Scurry, commander in Chief, in other words, exactly the same as prevailed during the first period of municipal authority, only giving him the rank of Brigadier-General, as of course is his proper title.

The collusion which the newspapers made much of between the militia and deputy sheriffs in which both parties arrested each other and it took some time in the city hall to straighten things out did not occur during my command, but may have after I had been relieved by the Chief of Police.

I not only received a particularly kind reception at Houston, but in Dallas, Captain O. Paget of the Dallas Rough Riders, who had done pretty good work under General Scurry's command, insisted upon receiving me with a military luncheon at the Oriental Hotel in Dallas, and insisted on giving me the Dallas Rough Riders, which were turned out in arms as a personal Guard of Honor and escorted me to the depot.[17] They made a great deal of noise in the passenger station but I appreciated their desire to treat me hospitably, and was accordingly grateful.

BEN C. STUART

Ben C. Stuart (1847–1929), born in Galveston, had a twenty-five year career on the staff of the Galveston Daily News. *In addition to his regular reporting, he also wrote and published historical sketches about the city. Although he survived the storm, his memoir, written approximately fourteen years later, comes across more as a newspaper account. In true reporter fashion, Stuart made every attempt to verify the time of the storm, the depth of the water, and other statistics that are difficult, if not impossible, to prove.*

THE GREAT GALVESTON DISASTER

On September 4th, 5th, 6th, 7th and 8th 1900 warnings were sent out by the Weather bureau at Washington that a West Indian hurricane was prevailing in the Gulf and cautioning ship masters against proceeding to sea. On September 8th the Galveston Weather Bureau forecasted high northerly winds that night, and accordingly the wind rose about 2 o'clock in the morning of the 8th blowing at first from the north but shifting to the eastward and at 6:15 [P.M.], it had attained a velocity of 84 miles an hour. For two minutes the velocity was at the rate of 100 miles an hour, when the anemometer blew away, but it was estimated by the observer at the weather bureau that prior to 8 p.m. the wind attained a velocity of 120 miles an hour.

About 8 p.m. when the wind shifted to the east there was a distinct lull, but when it again began to blow from the east and southeast, it appeared to have greater fury than before, but there were no means of computing the velocity. The wind shifted to the south about 11 p.m. on the 8th and steadily diminished in force. At 8 o'clock on the morning of the 9th the wind was from the south and was blowing at the rate of 26 miles an hour. The greatest hurricane ever experienced on the Texas coast was over.

Clarence Ousley, now the editor of the Fort Worth *Record*, but then the editor and one of the owners of the Galveston *Tribune* in his account of the hurricane says:

> The barometer began to fall on the afternoon of the 6th and continued to fall until the morning of the 8th when it read 29.42 inches. It fell more rapidly until 7 p.m. when it recorded 28.48 inches. An unofficial announce-

> ment from Washington declared this to be the lowest barometer in the history of the weather bureau. The tide had been boisterous for several days. The bathers had rare spell until Friday night, when the surf became too rough for comfort or safety.[18]

Saturday morning the waters rose over the lower parts of the city. The hurricane in the Gulf was depressing the water out at sea, and piling it by reaction upon the shore. But the north wind was so strong it did not encroach very far until noon. Meanwhile the tide had crept steadily into the harbor, and at 2 p.m. the gauge showed an elevation of six feet above mean low tide. The north wind reinforced the tide in the bay and drove the water angrily over the wharves and railway tracks. By three o'clock in the afternoon there had been a property damage to the railroad and shipping interests of more than one hundred thousand dollars. The last train arrived shortly after noon. Traffic was abandoned because the three railway bridges, across the two miles of West Bay, were submerged.

During the afternoon the water rose steadily, submerged many beachside residences, and wrecked a few. At 5 o'clock the tide was about nine feet above mean low and just covered the highest streets. After this hour observations are confusing and contradictory. Some men declare that the highest flood as at 7 to 8 p.m. and other declare that the tide was at the flood about midnight. All, however, agree that the subsidence was remarkably rapid. Some say half an hour, but the opinion of the calmest is that it left the streets in little more than an hour.

These contrary observations may be partly accounted for by the fact that many persons were without time pieces, or did not consult them, or that the experience during the flood seemed longer than the experience after the subsidence. But there was undoubtedly an inequality in the height of the water, and a considerable variation in the time of flood and of subsidence. These apparent anomalies may be accounted for by the fact that along the beach front the wrecked houses made a barrier of debris, more or less compact in certain places, which held back the water a while, and held it in longer; and especially by the plain geographical condition that the island slopes gently northward and southward from the central line of Broadway, running east and west, and when subsidence began the south wind assisted it in clearing the northern slope, while retarding it from flowing backward across the southern slope.

In the face of these weather warnings, and the rising tide, why, it may be properly asked, did the people not take refuge on the highest ground and in the best buildings? Many did. The district of total destruction contained 2,636 houses by actual map count. In these houses were from fifteen to sixteen thousand persons. One third, or one half, of them moved out Saturday afternoon. From noon to night the streets were thronged with refugees. By night flight was dangerous or impossible. The wind was doing murder with flying slate, and the angry waves were claiming their victims by the score.

Many were unafraid, or judged their houses sufficiently strong. This was not foolhardiness. There had been high waters before, notably in 1875 and 1886, when the effect was mainly discomfort and wrecked fences.[19] For years the physical geographers had argued plausibly, supported by experience, that the high water records were the maximum of possibility, because the beach at Galveston slopes so gently to the ocean depths, that destructive waves would be dissipated before reaching shore. Thus assured, many a man of intelligence and ordinary prudence surveyed the rising tide with perfect equanimity. The inundation would be wasteful and damaging, to be sure, but it brought no danger to high raised and stoutly built houses; had no terror for self possessed and reasoning persons. The wind grew hour by hour, and the tide rose inch by inch. Recollecting the comparative harmlessness of previous storms, it is not surprising that the people felt so little fear. Confidently expecting each minute to see abatement it is not strange that they were so calm and self-possessed. When the crisis came, their calmness and self-possession served them well; and they came through the experience from first to last complete masters of themselves.

WIDE SPREAD AREA OF DESTRUCTION

But all along the Gulf shore, with an ever widening path to the westward, until the destruction reached entirely across the suburban section covering an area of fifteen hundred acres, containing 2,636 houses, the havoc of wind and wave was complete. Here not a timber remains on the original site. The Gulf has now encroached on the land from a half a block to a block and to this extent the very sites are lost. The tall chimney

36. "The tall chimney of the old burned Beach Hotel lies a pile of brick on the edge of the water; and the stout piles on which the hotel rested now stand in the surf."—Ben C. Stuart

of the old burned Beach Hotel lies a pile of brick on the edge of the water; and the stout piles on which the hotel rested now stand in the surf.[20] The bath houses and amusement resorts along the beach, where thousands gathered in summer, are utterly obliterated. Elsewhere in the city at least a thousand more houses were broken to pieces or wrecked beyond repair. The total of absolute destruction was more than three thousand six hundred.

In this formless and endless wreckage were more than three thousand corpses. A thousand more were picked up in streets and yards. Five hundred more were picked up or picked to pieces by buzzards on the shores of the bay. Five hundred more were taken out by the receding tide, and fed the carrion fish of the deep sea. Even in October the death list swells daily and the known lost reach within a few hundred of six thousand.

Counting strangers, those who had lately arrived and had not yet made friends to inquire about and report them, and leaving as small margin for other unchronicled disappearances, it must be sure that the figures are conservative.

To this mortality in the city must be added ten or twelve hundred on the island to the west. The population outside the city on the island was, by the last census, sixteen hundred. The census taker, who lived twelve miles below, at the outer edge of the island community, and who knew practically all the residents of the district, estimates that not over four hundred remain. On the main land northward, in the coast counties for a swath of sixty miles wide, and one hundred north, by the most careful estimates there were at least a thousand more. The sum total of deaths by the hurricane of Sept 8th, therefore, was more than eight thousand. The maximum estimates are ten thousand to twelve thousand. The property damage in the city alone is variously estimated from twenty to thirty million dollars. These estimates, of course, included the damage to public, non-taxable property, such as paving, water-works, schools, and churches, and the damage to railroad terminals and shipping.

AFTER THE HURRICANE

For the first few hours on Sunday morning Sept 9th, the homeless sought shelter and food, as best they could. About 10 o'clock a hurried meeting of a dozen or more of the leading citizens was held and it was determined to get the news of the disaster to the outside world, to the President, the Governor and the newspapers. The only outlet was by means of boat across the bay. The three railroad bridges, and wagon bridge were destroyed. A twenty foot launch was secured and the messengers proceeded to Texas City, from whence they made their way on foot to the nearest point where the railway was intact, and securing a hand car proceeded to Houston, fifty miles distant from Galveston. From that place the news of the disaster and the cry for help was flashed to the outside world.

At 2 o'clock Sunday afternoon a citizens meeting was held and relief committees appointed. At that hour the general estimate of the dead was five hundred and it was questioned if the formality of a coroner's inquest should be suspended. This was soon dissipated, and the corpses were being assembled by scores at the temporary morgue on the north side of the Strand between 21st and 22nd streets. It was soon ascertained that, in most instances, identification was impossible, and that ordinary methods of interment were impracticable. There were seven hundred corpses in this morgue, of both sexes, white and black, Chinamen, Mexicans and in fact all nationalities to be found in the population of a busy seaport city.

It was determined to load the dead on barges, tow them to sea and cast them into the deep. This was done, and the gruesome spectacle then presented is one which none who were witnesses desire to see again. Many of these bodies were again cast ashore by the currents, and it was seen that some other method must be invoked. Burial on the spot where found, or incineration, generally the latter, were the only practicable methods, and they were pursued for more than six weeks. Huge piles of burning wreckage in which bodies of victims were being consumed, became such an usual spectacle, as to create no comment.

The local military companies had been called out to preserve order. There was some looting, but the remedy was swift and effective. Current reports were that as many as seventy-five ghouls had been shot in their backs. Diligent inquiry discloses the incorrectness of this report. It may be said that if any were killed it was not in excess of half a dozen. By

37. "It was determined to load the dead on barges, tow them to sea and cast them into the deep."—Ben C. Stuart

38. "Martial law was declared."—Ben C. Stuart

Tuesday morning every able bodied man was set to work, clearing the wreckage from the streets. Martial law was declared and Brigadier General Thomas Scurry, adjutant general of the state was placed in command, his force consisting of militia companies from the interior.

For the first few days after the hurricane, the most threatening condition was the absence of fresh water. Galveston derives its supply from artesian wells at Alta Loma, a station on the Gulf Colorado and Santa Fe railway, eighteen miles from the city, transmitted through a pipe line which, for two miles, crosses the bay. Fortunately there was no break in the 36-inch main, and there was no interruption in the flow. The stand pipe and the city reservoir were intact, but the pumping station had been wrecked. Mr. C. H. McMaster, a member of the Board of Water Commissioners, immediately set a force to work, and within a few days there was an abundant supply.[21] Five days after the hurricane, telegraphic communications had been restored, and by the 20th of September one of the railway bridges had been repaired, and traffic was resumed.

THOMAS L. MONAGAN

As a representative of Phoenix Assurance Company, a large insurance company that suffered heavy losses at Galveston, Monagan led a small group of men from Dallas to Galveston to learn the extent of his company's loss. The group arrived in Houston on Sunday, September 9th, the day after the storm, and volunteered to assist in the organization and running of a relief train bound for Galveston. All passengers on the train were required to have passes, which Monagan collected, confirming each person had correct credentials. He saved these passes until 1925, when he offered to return them to the individuals named in them.

His story appeared in the Dallas Morning News *on Sunday, June 7, 1925.*

We could not reach Virginia Point. The train was forced to halt some miles north of Texas City. But we were determined to reach Galveston to take them the message of cheer that help was on the way. Col. Sterrett, myself, and others of the Dallas group took off our shoes, rolled up our trousers legs and waded off into the water.[22]

We did not know what was ahead; we only knew that we must reach Galveston. We waded for miles, stumbling over dead stock and many times passing the bodies of drowned persons which had been swept inland from the coast. Finally, we reached Texas City. Ashore from the storm were two boats of some sort, tramp steamers, I believe. Gen. McKibben, without compunction, commandeered the only lifeboat in sight and loaded it with soldiers.[23] They started across the bay toward the stricken city, leaving the rest of us behind.

About this time we sighted a sailboat halfway across the bay, headed toward us. It was having trouble coming in, for the air was still in the calm which came after the storm had subsided. At last it came to the dock where we were. I had no authority beyond that which had been given me by Gen. McKibben on the train, but at the instance of Col. Sterrett I took charge of that boat, commandeered it, as it were. I learned its capacity and told off those of the group whom I desired to take with me.

We started. The trip across was filled with agony because of a lack of wind. We had to tack about every 100 yards. The bay was filled with bodies, with furniture, and with lumber. It must have taken us from four to four and a half hours to get within a half mile of the city. It was dark then, pitch dark, and looking toward the island we saw only one light in the whole place. It might have been the light of a watchman making his rounds; we never found it.

We approached the wharf and found it had collapsed. From it arose a terrible stench of dead animals and human beings. Some of those on the boat who had loved ones out there in the darkness climbed ashore and disappeared. But the rest believed it would be impossible to do anything or go anywhere in the dark, so we decided to pull out into the bay a little and anchor until daylight. All through the night, a night of horrible sounds, we remained there, 150 yards off shore.

At daybreak we pulled up the anchor and made for shore, entering the city at the foot of Twenty-third Street. [Col.] Sterrett was with me. We sighted a man hurrying past and stopped him to get information. This was Monday morning and as far as we know we were the first to reach the city from the outside world. The man told us of the thousands killed. It staggered us. Everywhere we looked was destruction wrought by wind and wave. It beggars description.

The islander also told us that bodies of the dead were being burned by hundreds to avoid an epidemic. Col. Sterrett could not believe what had been told us. "Surely," he said, "the man must be mistaken. It is always

39. "We approached the wharf and found it had collapsed."—Thomas Monagan

40. "They were bringing the bodies to the wharf on every kind of conveyance."
—Thomas Monagan

the rule to exaggerate these calamities and he is only repeating what some one has told him." But we investigated it and found it to be true. The authorities were piling up the bodies on the debris and setting fire to the whole mass.

The citizens who were unharmed had tried at first to gather up the dead at the regular mortuaries, but these had soon filled and still thousands of bodies were to be disposed of. So they had brought in abandoned barges to the wharf and loaded on them hundreds of bodies as they were pulled from the wreckage of destroyed buildings. Most of these were badly discolored and unrecognizable. They tied sash weights to their legs and threw them into the bay and came back for another load. They were bringing the bodies to the wharf on every kind of conveyance, but chiefly by fire trucks which had been pressed into service.

And to aid in the disposition of the bodies, human pyres were lighted in several places and hundreds were burned without identification. I have never told before about the burning of the bodies; it seemed too awful in a civilized country, but they were burning them.

We walked over the island, speechless at the sight of the prosperous city laid in waste. We were halted often by the guards, as the city was under martial law, but we had the proper credentials and were allowed to proceed. We went on into the business district and past the old Galveston News Building.[24] It was deserted and wide open. Wires about it were down and through the roof of a trolley car which had been halted by the tidal wave almost at the door of the News Building, a telephone pole had crashed its way.

Col. Sterrett was astounded at the sight of The News Building, deserted at that hour and at such a critical time. He said it was the first time he had ever known such a condition and that it was something that would never happen again. It was that incident which impressed the awfulness of the city's tragedy upon him. Ghouls already were at work robbing the dead and soldiers from the island fort shot several of them the day we arrived."

GORDON GAITHER

Gordon Gaither of Chilton, Texas, wrote to Thomas Monagan after learning that he was returning the original passes to the men named in them. His letter appears with the unreturned passes in the Rosenberg Library's collection.

JUNE 8, 1925

My Dear Sir: I read your article appearing in Sunday's Dallas News in which you state you have the passes of those that went to Galveston on the first relief train out of Houston to carry aid to the stricken city after the storm of Sept 1900. I was on that train as you know from my pass and I am writing to ask that you kindly send me my pass as I desire to keep it as a memento of that awful trip.

I read your very accurate account of that trip with much interest. I remember distinctly all the incidents you mention. I had a sister and aunt in Galveston at the time of the storm. My aunt was Matron of the Rosenberg Orphan's Home and my sister was teacher in same.[25]

As you state it was night when our boat reached Galveston, and I never will forget the one lone flickering light that we saw on the Island. You will remember part of us landed that night and walked ashore on the narrow frame work, this being all that was left of the wharf. I landed at night because I was anxious to know the fate of my sister and aunt. Of course you know what a gruesome sight met our gaze and it was made more appalling because it was night.

Early next morning I went forth to find my sister and aunt. I walked up to the Orphans Home and found that part of the building had collapsed and nobody around there at all. However, I finally found them in a nearby frame building where they had taken the children after the Storm subsided, without the loss of a life. Fortunately they all happened to be in the part of the building that stood.

I have occasion to remember my five mile walk from where we got off the train to Texas City. I was wearing a new pair of shoes and when I reached Texas City I could hardly walk my feet hurt so badly. When we left Houston, my friend W. D. Thomas and I neglected to carry any food with us, we had only a Gal. bottle of water, and this is all we had, except we begged a few crackers from some fellow on the boat while crossing the Bay.

DESTRUCTION OF GALVESTON ORPHANS' HOME

41. Galveston Orphans' Home. "I walked up to the Orphans Home and found that part of the building had collapsed and nobody around there at all." —Gordon Gaither

Please pardon me for writing such a lengthy letter, but I know a man who was thoughtful enough to keep those passes all these years and return them to those who used them on that memorable trip is all right and will not mind taking a little time to read a long letter from one who accompanied him.

Yours very truly
Gordon Gaither

LOUISA HANSEN ROLLFING

Louisa Christina Hansen Rollfing was born in 1859 in Nieblum on the Frisian Island of Foehr in Germany and came to America in 1880 to live with family in Lake Charles, Louisiana. She moved to Galveston in 1883 and married August Rollfing, a painter, just weeks after surviving the 1885 fire. At the time of the 1900 storm they had three children: Helen, August, and Atlanta. She wrote her memoir in 1932 at the age of seventy-two at their request. In it, she describes how angry she was with her husband for taking the approaching storm so lightly. Could it have been woman's intuition that provided her with a sense of impending doom?

Her comments about not seeing any dead people on the way from Julia's house to Grandma's are surely incorrect. No other account fails to mention the scores of dead bodies lying everywhere. It is possible that she carefully mentioned not seeing corpses to avoid being coarse or crude at the end of that Victorian age. Perhaps, thirty-two years later, she simply did not want to dwell on the unpleasant sights.

This account, along with Sarah Davis Hawley's letter, is one of the few that go into great detail about cleaning specific items or rooms following the storm. These were chores that showed how much work simply had to be done to make conditions livable.

During the night of September 8th the wind was blowing very strong and reports of a storm in the Gulf were heard.[26] But no one was alarmed more than at any other time when we heard these reports. Everybody went about their business in the same way as on any other Saturday.

August at that time was painting the Trust Building, and was nearly finished with his work there, so he left as usual at 7:30 to attend to his business. At 9 o'clock the rain poured down in streams. Driftwood came down the street, and the wind got stronger and stronger every minute. For a while even ladies were wading in the water, thinking it was *fun*. The children had a grand time, picking up driftwood and other things that floated down the street. They went near the beach and told us that the bathhouses were breaking to pieces. Then it wasn't fun anymore. People began to vacate their homes, and went farther into town to safer places.

I sent August [son] to town in the street car, to make his father come home and take us away too. Water was already coming in over the door-sill.[27] August told his father, "Mama says to come home she wants to move." So he came back (the street cars were still running). "Papa says, 'You must be crazy', he will come home for dinner."

The water was coming in more and we were all so scared. I saw more of the neighbors leave, and time seemed so long before he finally came, it was after 12 o'clock—and was surprised there wasn't any dinner. I hadn't even thought about cooking, so we both were mad. He told me to go upstairs with the children and he would go back to town and pay off his men, and then come back to us.

That was more than I could stand. I stamped my foot and said some terrible things. I told him, if he didn't go immediately and get a carriage to take us away, and we in the meantime would drown, it would be *his* fault and he would never have any peace, etc. I have never before and never after been so angry.

I believe I scared August, and he rushed right off and do, as I wanted him to do. Finally after 1 o'clock a buggy came, with a nigger to drive—that was all he could get in a livery stable at Malloy's.[28]

I had packed shoes and suits for all of us in a hamper but in the buggy wasn't room for anything, so I had to leave it behind too. We got all in, I, the three children, and the driver, and started out towards the west end to get to Grandma's house. I had told August I wanted to go there, for surely we would be *safe* there.

It was a terrible trip, we could only go slowly for the electric wires were down everywhere, which made it so dangerous. I must give the driver credit for being as careful as he could be. The rain was icy cold and hurt our faces like glass splinters, and little 'Lanta' cried all along the way. I pressed her little face hard against my breast, so she would not be hurt so badly. August and Helen didn't cry, they never said a word.

We got as far as 40th Street and Ave. H, just one block from Grandma.

42. August Rollfing, Jr. "I sent August to town in the street car, to make his father come home and take us away."
—Louisa Rollfing

The water was so high, we just sat in it, the horse was up to his neck in water. We tried to turn down 40th Street, when some one shouted: "Don't go! You can't go through, it is too deep—there is a deep hole!"

So we turned around. "Where shall I go now?" the driver asked me. "I don't know, where could I go with my children?" Then I thought about Julia and Jim, August's sister. She lived on 36th and Broadway in a two story house. I decided to go there and see if she would take us in.

When she opened the door and saw us like drowned rats, she screamed: "My God! Louisa, what is the matter?" I told her how it was in the east end, and that we could not get through in the west end—she was glad to take us in. Jim was home.

I had $1 in my pocket, gave it to the driver, and thanked him for his careful driving. I made him promise to leave word with Mr. Malloy for my husband to let him know where he could find us.

I was so confident that August would go there, but he did not. It seemed, that Julia and Jim were quite unaware of the condition, but when I told them what I had seen on the way they too were alarmed and nervous and scared.

We got into some dry things, and took our clothes and shoes out into her wash house. We nailed ironing boards and table boards across outside doors and windows and secured everything as good as possible. A neighbor with her two children asked to be taken in. So we were 10 altogether in the house. The storm got worse and worse and the water came in under the doors—and soon rose higher. We had closed all the doors upstairs that led into the hall, and sat on the stairs as high as possible. We had taken a pitcher of water along and a railroad lantern so we weren't exactly in the dark.

We heard soon the blinds and windows break in the rooms upstairs, and the sound in those rooms is not easy to describe. It sounded, as if the rooms were filled with a thousand little devils, shrieking and whistling. In the rooms downstairs the furniture, even the piano, slid from one side of the rooms to the other and then back again. The water was up above the doors now, over seven feet and if it kept rising more we would not be able to escape. We all prayed!

August, Helen and Fay and the other two children would say, "Let us pray again, maybe God has time now to hear us." Julia cried, and begged Jim to get out somehow and try to get across the street to Reyder's place.[29] It was a desperate idea and Jim told her they never could do it, because the water was much higher there than where they were, so they did not try. I believe though, she consented mostly because I was there with our children, and of course it was out of the question for me to do anything, except *stay*.

All at once something cracked. The kitchen broke loose from the house, and left a big opening. It did not make much difference, as the house was full of water anyway. Soon after, the house was lifted off the brick pillars on two sides and now was hanging slanting. I think it was about 12 o'clock when the water fell. We could see more and more of the doors, and it was marvelous how fast it went down. We knew then, that the worst was over.

Where was our dear Papa!? During these terrible hours I never thought that he was in much danger, or that he even might be dead. I had reconciled myself to the thought, that the children and I might be drowned, but he was so big and strong and only himself to take care of so he surely would be all right.

At 4 o'clock someone pounded on the front door, and in came August and his brother, Fred. When he saw us all, he said, "Thank God!" and fell just up the stairs, and laid there for a while without moving. He was more dead than alive.

When he told us later of his experience and exposure thru the night, we felt, as if we had been sheltered. After he had sent the buggy for us, he went to his shop and waited for his men to come to get their money, but not one of the 18 men he had working came. He watched for a while, and saw the tin roofs of buildings tear loose, roll up and fly through the air. Boards and glass was hurled everywhere.

He locked his shop and started to follow us out to his mother's. If he only had gone to Malloy's as I expected he would, it would have been so much better. Then he would have known where he could find us. He got as far as the Waterworks, on 30th Street, when the wind picked him up and tumbled him around like a piece of paper, through the water, up on the sidewalk. He got his arm around a telephone pole and held on to that. When a lull came in the wind he crawled up to the building and they let him in. The place was full of people who sought safety there.

In a short time it got too dangerous to stay there, the big smokestack began swaying and the people were afraid to be killed that way, so they got out and then it was everybody for himself. August and two big negroes held on together, and got into a grocery store. In a little while they had to leave that place, and got into an open house. A big beam fell and killed a man in the water. So these three men held together and went on, then they saw a light in another store, the people inside at last let them in, at first they did not want to open the door, but they finally did. The water was so high, that all the people stood on the counters, about 80 people were there, men, women, and children. August held a little boy on his shoulder for a long time.

All at once one man hollered, "The water is going down, look at the door!" And it rapidly fell, just as we watched it go down at Julia's house. The storekeeper pulled out a jug of whiskey and gave them all a drink, men and women alike. They all needed it, I am sure.

Now August started out again to get to his mother's where he was so

43. Galveston Waterworks. "In a short time it got too dangerous to stay there, the big smokestack began swaying."—Louisa Rollfing

sure to find us. But what a way to tread! Houses and fences were lying across the streets everywhere, deep holes in the ground, and dark everywhere. He stumbled and fell again and again, got up and get a few paces, and fall again.

It was three o'clock when he saw the little house, without fences or anything. It was about the only house in the neighborhood left whole, all the others were so badly damaged or gone altogether, some were just drifted a few blocks towards the Bay, across railroad tracks. These were moved back later.

But the worst was yet to come. After his question, "Where are Louisa and the children? I don't see them." And his mother told him, "August, I don't know. They are not here, my boy. I haven't seen them. When did they go, and how?" "At 1 o'clock in a buggy." "Nobody could come here at 1 o'clock. Wait August, wait until daylight." "No, I am going *now!* Oh where can they be? Maybe at Mary's, maybe at Julia's. I am going!" "I am going with you," said Fred, and then again, out in the rain and storm.

They passed Mary's house, nobody there, then on to Julia's, where at

4 o'clock he found us. We were together and nothing else mattered. If I had seen him struggle through all this hardship, I think I would have died or lost my mind.

And yet this was only our experience, we did not know of all the horrors and deaths that had taken place in Galveston in this terrible night. After hearing all this, we tried to make some coffee, which was a hard enough task, as everything was so wet. When finally it was made, we could not drink it, it was so salty. All the water in the cisterns was ruined from the salt spray.

It got to be daylight and we saw that the house was a complete wreck and totally unsafe to stay in. The wash house was gone, so was the kitchen—our shoes and clothes we never saw again—so we had only the things Julia had lent us. Julia took possession of a little house across the street, which was vacant and had not suffered so much which was very fortunate for her.

After a little rest August went off to see how it looked our way. He said, "If I can find a dry spot to lie down, I won't come back right away, so don't worry." He went out on Tremont Street, which was not quite so bad, but when he came as far as Ave. N, he could not get any further. Here was a barricade as high as a two story house, seemingly endless toward the east and west. House upon house, all broken to pieces, furniture, pianos, sewing machines, cats and dogs. And what was underneath? Nobody knew yet, how many people had gone down with their houses, was yet a closed book.

In a round about way he came at last to the area where we had lived, what did he find there? Nothing! Absolutely nothing! The ground was as clear of anything as if it had been swept, not even a little stick of wood or anything; for blocks and blocks nothing and then that terrible pile of debris, and what was in and under it.

So he did not find a *dry spot,* and in a couple of hours came back, loaded down with groceries, a big ham and bread, all he possibly could carry. We had no home to go back to, and could not stay where we were. We left Julia and started out toward Grandma's house, that at least had a roof over it. It was hard to get there, even in day time, the streets were all blocked with broken houses, fences, etc., and deep holes with water in the ground. On the edge of one of these holes little August slipped and went in, the groceries were dropped and Papa succeeded in pulling him out, he could easily have drowned.

44. "The ground was as clear of anything as if it had been swept . . . for blocks and blocks nothing and then that terrible pile of debris."—Louisa Rollfing

The sun was shining beautifully and the wind had died down. Dead cats and dogs and chickens were lying everywhere, but we did not see any dead people on our way.[30]

His mother's house was really the only one holding together in that neighborhood, and we think Grandpa Vieman had done a good job building it so very strong, if not very pretty.[31] You haven't any idea about the filth in the house. The water of course had been high in the rooms, and soaked everything and when it got down left a *scum* over everything. All the bedding was covered with it, and some stuffed furniture were all soaked with it, and soon began to smell terrible. We just carried it all outdoors, there wasn't any water to wash the bedding, so we had to dry it and stand the smell. We scrubbed the walls and floors the best we could, but on account of the scarcity of water we could not do much. I cried bitterly when I thought about my lovely household and not have one single thing, not even a stitch of clothing for my children. I just did not know what to do.

Then Mama scolded me and said, "We should be glad, that we were all living." I saw that she was right, but nevertheless it was hard not to know what to do next. I haven't any recollection what we had on, but I know little August had a dress, and Lanta had a long red dress which I made shorter, so she could walk.

August just bought groceries and we hid them up in the attic so nobody could find them. The first time he came home from town he told us that at least a hundred people had drowned; that sounded awful, and we could not believe it. In another day we knew that several *thousand* people were missing, and the number grew from day to day. The exact number never was known.

The bridge to the mainland was destroyed and telegraph communication was cut off. We were isolated from the outside world. People wanted to leave in large numbers, as everybody was afraid of an epidemic, but for days that was impossible.

The most necessary thing was to dispose of the *dead.* At first they tried to bury some, but this was not possible. August was never forced to help with this gruesome work, as there were many men who could not be helpful in any other way. Willie and Fred both had to help with the dead.[32]

I went to town one day to get me a pair of slippers, I just could not go barefooted, and I wish you could have seen me. I still had Julia's shoes, and they were so large that I had to stuff them full of rags to hold them on my feet. I had on Mama's sunbonnet, it was so hot. It was hotter that year than ever before in September, which made the smell so much worse. I never did *see* a corpse as I never left the house to go *sight seeing.* I saw a big *truck* coming past me, and when I turned to get out of the way, I saw a leg and an arm stick out under the tarpaulin. I knew then that it was loaded with *dead bodies.* August had told me, they were carried way out in the Gulf by the boat load and dumped there as the *only* way to dispose of them, to save the living. It made me sick, when I saw that truck; I knew what it meant. But even this did not work. The bodies floated back in a terrible condition. The only possible way was to burn them, and all along the beach were fires built for that purpose, and burned day and night.

Very few people were identified. Whole families were gone. In some instances the father was saved, in some the mother, and in some little children were miraculously saved. When I heard all this, I did not complain or grieve about losing all our possessions. Yes, we were lucky we did not lose *one* in the whole family. How few people could say that. I know of families where as many as 18 relatives were lost. So God had been good to us.

A few days later, August and the three children were asleep in this fashion: a mattress was placed on the floor, all the heads in the center and the bodies sprawled every which way, wherever they could find room. I had to squeeze in somewhere. I was not sleepy, so decided to write home, and tell Father and Mother the terrible news. I wrote a very long letter and never stopped, reading it over, closed it, and in the morning August sent it off, so that was off my mind, and I forgot about it.

I told you about the wall of debris as high as a two-story house around the east end, it would have taken weeks to remove it and burn it. So they gave up looking for dead bodies and just burned it in sections. Oh how many dead ones will have been buried this way, and the living friends or relatives never knew, but it was the only way.

The fear of epidemic was keen, and the Mayor and Aldermen tried to make as many ladies and children as possible leave Galveston. The railroad between Houston and Texas City had been repaired and barges would take them across the Bay from Galveston. A great many left, as one could have free transportation to any place in the United States. My relatives in Lake Charles, Mina and Diedrich Jessen, wired as soon as telegrams could be sent, even wired me $25.00 and wanted us *all* to come.

After we had been ten days at Grandma's we thought it best, for me and the children to go for a while. Poor Grandma, I know she was tired of it, it was so crowded and miserable, and would be a relief to be alone. I don't blame her in the least. I helped all I could, but we were so handicapped in everything.

August was awful busy, and could not get men enough to do the work; at first it was only putting in skylights and window panes in houses and big buildings, so far it had not rained which in a way was a blessing. If we went away, he could sleep in his shop, and take his meals in a restaurant, and would save so much time and save his strength. So I had to get ready.

I went to town and bought us each a pair of shoes, Helen and Lanta a little dress and August a pair of pants and a shirt, belt and tie, myself a shirtwaist. The children did not get any hats, but *I* had to have a *hat!* I went into a west end store kept by a Jewess and asked for hats. Yes, she had some. I picked out a gray felt hat, with a little band of black ribbon fastened with little buckles, it looked all right. I asked for a looking glass, and I wish you could have seen her. She rolled her eyes and threw her hands over her head. "A looking glass, who cares now for a looking glass?" "I do, do you think I spend a whole dollar for a hat and don't know if it looks good on me? I am going to wear this hat all winter!" So she got one and I got my hat. I know she thought I was crazy.

We had a big dog named Dewey before the storm and I left him upstairs with my little canary before we left the house, and of course did not know how they died. About three days after the storm August met a man he knew well at his hardware store, his home was on Avenue L.

"Rollfing, there is a trunk with your wife's name in the debris before our house, and a dog by it. He is living, but in a terrible weakened condition. He doesn't want to eat or drink." "Oh that is Dewey!" So August hurried out there, and the dog knew him but was so weak he could not stand or walk.

The lady told him the trunk was closed, but not locked, so she opened it and spread the contents on the wood to dry. I had packed all our winter clothes, overcoats and dresses we did not wear through the summer—even my new portieres.[33] She said a crowd of niggers passed and each grabbed something, August's winter suits, coats, and overcoat before she could stop them. My things they left alone.

August had to carry Dewey in his arms to town, and took him to a restaurant and ordered him a big steak. It is a wonder he did not die after being starved for days. Then he brought him home. We gave him a warm bath and medicine. Every one of us cried when we saw him, but could not touch him. He had the mange so bad, so we had to be careful. I left him with August in the shop when we left, and when we came back he looked fine.

I don't remember how we got down to the barge, but I guess we walked it, but I know how it was when we got *on* it. A railing of boards was nailed all around and in this enclosure we all stood like cattle in a pen. It was packed with women and children. I begged August to drink plenty of whiskey, and he promised cheerfully he would do it. That sounds funny, doesn't it.

By this time so much sickness from fever and dysentery caused by heat, bad water and decay was in Galveston. Doctors and nurses and disinfectants were inadequate, that anyone who could drink and get whiskey had a better chance to keep from getting sick. Therefore I told August to drink plenty of whiskey.

In Houston we were all taken to Turner Hall and registered. When the lady in charge saw my name, she said, "Oh, are you Mrs. Rollfing?" "Yes." "Then I must send somebody with you to Mr. Juenger's home, she has been anxious about you.[34] You can leave the children here, we will take good care of them."

A man went with me to Juenger's home, when I met Mrs. Juenger for the first time. After question after question about August and conditions in Galveston, he dressed and took me back to Turner Hall, where supper was ready for everybody. We took the children and went to a nice restaurant where we had a grand supper at a private table. He was so happy that we were all saved, and wanted us to stay with them in Houston. I thanked him, but said I was on my way to Lake Charles where our relatives wanted us.

It was then about train time and he bought bags of fruit for the children and tucked a $5.00 bill in August's pocket. I did not know this until we were on the train and on our way.

I don't remember much about the trip, we were all tired and I had so much to think about, that I don't even remember who met us. We went to Jessen's house and everybody was crying when they saw us. After the children were put to bed I walked across the room and Mina began to laugh. I did not know the reason and asked her, "What is so funny?" I did not feel like laughing. And felt, as if I *never* could laugh any more.

She got up and pulled me before a big mirror, and turned me around. "Look, Louisa!" No wonder she laughed. It was my skirt. It was style then to wear your skirts real long with a little short train about 6 or 7 inches in the back. And as this was a nice going out skirt, I had made it according to style. It had shrunk so in my trunk, that now my little train hung like a nice little tail in the back. I had to laugh. Here I had gone through Houston, to the restaurant, and everywhere, my little tail hanging down. The next morning I made it even.

All the other relatives came flocking in to see us and hear the details of the Storm. I got very tired of repeating the same sad story. The children were happy, but as yet did not have any clothes to wear. The next morning we made our plans. We were a very well organized family.

I started sewing as fast as I could. I made underwear for all of us out of the bolt of domestic and dresses for the girls and shirts for August, a wrapper for me and a shirtwaist of the red Percale. I got tired of looking at red. Then I got a bright idea! I asked the girls, "Don't you think this is a pretty pattern?" "Yes, it is." "Would you like to have a waist out of it?" "Yes, I would." "All right, you buy me another piece and I give you this."

This way I got some different waists and August some striped shirts. I do think I had a bright idea. I was beginning to feel like myself. Only, underneath was always the worry, would August keep well? Without anybody to care for him? He assured me on postcards that he was feeling well and was very busy. I had to be contented until there was a chance to rent some rooms in Galveston.

After I had been there a month, August wrote for us to come back to Galveston, we could have rooms now. We were all happy, but I didn't have any idea how we would manage, but time would tell.

We came home on Sunday afternoon and the pleased look on August's face when he saw us dressed so nicely, so different, from the way we looked when we left a month before. We walked around a while, talking, and did not seem to be bound for anywhere. I finally asked, where our rooms were. He looked kind of sheepish. "We will have to bunk in the shop tonight, and tomorrow you have all day to look around. I am so busy all day and can't take time. I just could not stand it any longer to be alone."

I felt sorry for him and said, "It's all right, August."

ARNOLD R. WOLFRAM

In 1900 Arnold R. Wolfram lived with his wife, Mary, and four of their six children ranging in age from six to sixteen at 1414 Twenty-ninth Street (between Avenue M½ and Avenue N). He was employed as a salesman by Arthur B. Jones, who ran a fruit and produce store at Twenty-third and Strand.

Wolfram wrote his account in September 1939. Its beginning illustrates changes in memories and attitudes with the passage of time. According to the official U.S. Weather Bureau journal, the storm warning flag was raised on September 7, 1900. Wolfram, thirty-nine years later, seems to recall it being set out for 'several days' instead of the Friday before.

Saturday, September 8th, 1900 dawned as any other morning, however anxiety was in every heart and apprehension as to what the day would bring forth. Storm warnings had been posted for several days and every one was urged to prepare. Galveston had no protecting seawall at that time and an impending storm of the magnitude of the one predicted was enough to make the stoutest heart quail.

I left for the office at the usual time. My family pleaded with me to remain at home, but I was determined to go to town. I tried to reassure them and promised that at the first signs of the storm's approach, I would return home. Galveston was very small at that time and my business was only twenty short blocks from our home. At the office we prepared for any emergency by putting all stock and office equipment on high shelves. It had been raining off and on all morning and a slight wind had been blowing.

Noon arrived and I lunched at home, but left again for my business, despite the tearful pleadings of my wife and children. Shortly after noon, the wind suddenly increased in velocity and steadily became stronger. The rain set in in earnest and came down in a veritable deluge. I rushed to close up my store thinking only of getting home to my family, but even though it seemed to have taken me only a moment, when I reached the street the wind was now a gale.

The rain slashed furiously and water was rushing in torrents in the gutter. Protecting myself as best I could, I prepared to start for home, now twenty long blocks away. I had bought a pair of shoes during the day and unconsciously as I left my store I picked up the package. I now thought of something. Standing in the shelter of a doorway, I unwrapped my shoes, tied them together and fastened them to my head.

Slate and glass were flying through the air and I felt this precaution might help. Once again I started out. At the corner I suddenly stopped in horror. A little Western Union messenger boy, a lad of about ten years, had fallen from his wheel into the street and was being swept by the water towards the sewer drain. Even as I started toward him, he was just going into the whirlpool marking the spot of the drain. I caught him just in time, and dragged him up on the sidewalk.

I recognized him as a child who lived very near me, and shouted to him above the roar of the wind and rain that I would take him home. I then made him understand that it would be best if he took off his shoes and place them on his head as I had placed mine. And then we started forward.

We were now forcing our way in the very face of the storm, which had become a raging tempest. It was almost impossible to shout above the din, and I realized then that we were facing death. It didn't seem humanly possible that we could fight our way in the very teeth of this demon but somehow the thought of my family and what their fate might be, drove me on. I knew that I had to keep on, whether I reached my destination or not. By much shouting and gesticulating during momentary lulls, I made the little lad understand that he was to hold tight to my hand and should either of us fall that we must not clutch at the other. And so we started towards our goal: home, family and safety.

We now had six blocks to cover west, which was directly facing the storm. The wind and rain were wreaking havoc everywhere, poles and wires were snapping, making passage down the street doubly dangerous; windows were crashing in; flimsy structures and parts of roofs were swirling swiftly down the river which had, just a few hours before, been a beautiful esplanaded street; and the water was rising higher every minute.[35]

I realized that we would have to swim across this river, the sooner the better. After a nightmare of terror, we made it and then slowly worked our way for a block by the assistance of an iron picket fence.[36] As we neared the corner, we saw a man, faint and weak from exhaustion, holding to the fence. We did our best to hurry to his assistance, but before we could get to him, he loosed his hold and was lost.

We struggled slowly for another block and came to our beautiful Rosenberg monument to the heroes of Texas; here vehicles, debris of all sorts, was wedged in a tight mass.[37] We managed again to cross the street and traversed another block, by this time the water had risen until it was under our arm pits, and to make matters worse it was growing dark.

45. Galveston Artillery Club. ". . . we . . . slowly worked our way for a block by the assistance of an iron picket fence."—Arnold R. Wolfram

On this corner was the home of an old friend of mine and as we paused for a moment in the front of his house for a rest before attempting to cross another intersection, I looked up and saw him at his window. I called and tried in vain to attract his attention.

Later I learned that he had not seen me due to the dusk and rain. However, I learned that up until that time, he had been watching for any one in distress and would throw a rope to them, dragging them into his home. He had saved quite a number of people in this manner.

After we had decided that he had not seen or heard us, we began our struggle across to the opposite corner. Here was the home of another old friend, Mr. E. E. Rice.[38] But here, we suddenly encountered a terrific current. We were both suddenly swept from our feet and rushed pell-mell into a tree. I struggled up to the surface all the while holding frantically to the tree.

When I did reach the top, I discovered that my companion had miraculously saved himself in the same way. The tree wasn't very large but had several branches that would bear weight. We were pretty worn out by this time, so with a last ounce of strength, we both managed to haul ourselves into the fork of the branches.

The air was full of flying wood and slate and glass and the water was hurling everything imaginable at our perch. During this time, darkness had descended, but we sat in our tree and prayed that we might be spared. The moon shown faintly and we could almost distinguish objects going by. No doubt this was to our advantage, as we were able to protect ourselves from objects rushing by in the water; however, I sometimes wish the moon had stayed behind a cloud, for suddenly, whirling towards us was the roof of a house and clinging on the top was a man and woman.

The little raft crashed against our tree, hung there a moment and then parted, the man being carried away on one half. The other half was caught for a moment by other wreckage and the woman stretched out her hand to me and, screaming above the din, begged me to save her. I leaned out as far as I dared, my little companion keeping a fast grip on me and on his limb. The woman did her best to reach my hand, but suddenly the jam broke loose and she was swept under and away. I can still see her anguished face before me, can still hear her cries ringing in my ears.

Our own situation was becoming more desperate. I did not know how much longer we could rest securely in this tree, with the constant pressure of refuse piled against it. And too we were pretty tired, cold, hungry and sleepy. Then suddenly a long rafter of some sort became wedged tightly between our tree and the porch of my friend's home. I thought quickly: If the rafter would hold tight for a few minutes, by placing it between us and the oncoming torrent, we might make our way to the house.

But there was no time to lose, so grasping the boy and lowering him into the water, and the little tad seemed to have understood without a word from me, we frantically splattered our way to the porch and entered into a haven of warmth and peace. My friend's wife took in our condition in a glance and immediately went to work on the child, her husband taking me in charge. A brisk rubdown, some warm dry clothes and hot food made a wonderful change. And then a soft couch to lie down and rest.

The boy dropped off to sleep almost at once, but I could not sleep for thinking that here was I safe and sound, but where was my family? We had reached Mr. Rice's home about midnight, and between then and the morning, the storm gradually wore itself out, and the water began to recede. As soon as it was light and I knew that all danger had passed I thanked my kind friend for his hospitality and started out alone to see if I could find my wife and children. As I stepped off the sidewalk into the street, I stepped on something rather soft that gave way and nearly threw me down. I reached down under the water and discovered I had stepped on the stomach of a dead woman. I turned away sick and horrified, but as I walked on, again and again, I saw bodies of men, women and children, everywhere.

It's a sight I hope I shall never see again. Destruction and desolation; wreckage strewn everywhere, chaos, and that voice still ringing in my ears: "Save me, save me!" And at last I approached the block in which I lived. I dreaded to look but finally did—Oh my God, where would I find my loved ones—for I saw that my home was tilted crazily, the roof crushed in. I stood stunned, sickened to the very core of my being. Finally I started forward for I knew that no matter what I might find on reaching the house, I had to search those ruins of all I had held dear.

I had no more than taken two or three steps, when I heard someone calling me. It turned out to be a friend who had started out to look for me in behalf of my family. He assured me that my family was safe and sound, but that they felt as if they would never [see me again.]

You can imagine the wild joy when we all met again. I, of course, had to tell them of my terrible experiences. They, in turn, told how they had

46. ". . . I saw that my home was tilted crazily, the roof crushed in."
—Arnold R. Wolfram

to leave our home, when it began to shake and sway, how they made their way to the corner grocery on the next corner. Their experience through that nightmare of horror is a story worth telling, too, but would take much too long.

Over 8000 people were killed in the storm and the damage to the city was tremendous. My business was completely washed away and practically everything else we had. We did salvage most of our furniture. Our house was not damaged as much as it could have been for the cistern we had kept the house from falling over entirely. I later returned to the scene of my struggle in the tree and find the tree still standing. I immediately cut it down and took it home for a souvenir. The little lad whom I saved is now grown and married and has a very good business in another state but we still correspond.

I am now passed my 80th birthday and soon approaching my 81st. All my children have grown up, married, and have children of their own. And I even have some few great-grandchildren. But with all the changes of the years, that one night has always remained most vivid in my mind.

HENRY CORTES

Henry Cortes, born in November, 1893, to H.W. and Mary Cortes, lived with his older brothers and sisters in Houston. He wrote this memoir in 1957 before reading John Edward Weems's book, A Weekend in September.

By way of background, I am noting the following. September 8, the day of the hurricane, was my grandmother Cortes' birthday. Grandfather Henry Cortes' home in Galveston was on Avenue N at the corner of 32nd Street, about 14 blocks north of the Gulf of Mexico beach.[39] The household was made up of my grandparents, an unmarried daughter, Anna, and another daughter and her husband, Mr. and Mrs. C. J. Michaelis.[40]

On September 8, 1900, I was eight years old—less two months and three days. My father decided his mother's birthday and Saturday combined made an ideal time for a Galveston visit. So early that morning he, Mother and I, and other kin, caught the train for Galveston. I remember being dressed in the conventional youngster garb of the times—high-laced black shoes, black cotton stockings above the knees held by black elastic garters, white starched linen (or cotton) pants which hung a little below the knees, with a matching sailor-like long sleeved blouse, and a stiff "straw katy" hat.

As the day coach train rolled over the wooden trestle above Galveston Bay, we noted that choppy waves were already lapping at the ties and rails of another railroad trestle, as well as at the roadway of the wooden wagon bridge. This meant the tide was already several feet above normal. (It's hard to realize there were no autos or trucks then.)

When we got off the train at Galveston around 9 a.m., the station master got all the passengers together. He announced that a bad storm was scheduled to hit shortly and that the train on the next track would pull out for Houston right away. And further, it would be the last train to Houston until the storm was over. More than half of the passengers plus others already in Galveston promptly boarded the train. One aunt returned and there may have been others from our party, but my father being a hardheaded native elected to stay. (Note—all the railroad trestles and the wagon bridge were washed out during the hurricane.)

After we went through the depot to board a streetcar, my "straw katy" hat was blown away by the already gusty wind and was not recovered. At

47. Mallory line vessel grounded where the wagon bridge stood. ". . . all the railroad trestles and the wagon bridge were washed out."—Henry Cortes

the time we arrived at Grandmother's house there was only rain water in the streets from blustery showers. Soon after lunch the pre-hurricane tidal water was around 2½ feet deep and the winds were stronger. Even so, the neighboring kids were out playing in washtubs or homemade rafts. Sad to state, some were not alive the next day.

Grandfather's house was built about 1875, and an inspection in the summer of 1956 showed it still had sturdy oversized lumber in fine shape and of a quality that probably could not be found in lumber yards today. The house was what was called a "raised cottage" and is similar to the present one story and a half Cape Cod style. The one exception being that this wooden structure sits on, and is tied to, a *brick* foundation about

1½ feet thick and extending 8½ feet above the ground surface. (Many Galveston houses were built in this way but with *wooden* substructures and were washed away or broken to pieces with consequent loss of life.) After getting the family to Grandmother's house, my father went to town to visit my uncle Charlie Michaelis, who was co-owner of Star Drug Store. (This retail drug store still exists in the same name under other ownership on Tremont Street downtown next door to the corner where it originally was.)[41] When the tidal water became dangerous, they closed the drug store and set out on foot for home. They obtained four brooms, and after cutting off part of the straw, used one in each hand as support. My recollection is of seeing them struggling through about 3 to 4 feet of water as they got near the house.

Galveston people must have drunk lots of mineral water in those days, for my druggist uncle Charlie Michaelis bought such water by the carload and stored the wooden-cased glass bottles in his home basement. Late in the afternoon the menfolk boarded up the windows and doors outside and inside, and then piled the cases of mineral water as a strong support.

Shortly after dark it sounded as though all hell had broken loose. The hurricane winds caused intermittent roars as they blew in gusts greater than the steady velocities. The rains came in torrents, worked through the shingles of the roof and caused bulges and then breaks in the ceiling wallpaper and cloth that popped like a firecracker above the storm roar, thoroughly soaking everyone and everything. We were unable to see the lightning but we did hear it crackle and then heard the loud thunder claps that followed. Was I scared? My memory is very good that I was *plenty* scared, what with the pandemonium along with the wailing and praying of the women.

The men cut a hole about a foot square in one or more of the rooms. The idea was that if the open basement water came higher than the floor, the water could come in and help anchor the house to the brick foundation. This would then prevent the house from floating off or breaking to pieces. Every few minutes a 3-foot wooden rule was lowered in the hole and the time and the water depth below the floor were recorded with pencil and paper.

Oil lamps and candles were on hand and used, as the electric system had gone out. Early in the afternoon two bath tubs and every pot and pan were filled with fresh water and covered to keep the salt water out.

Rope had been obtained and was cut for use by each man in connection with the women and children he was to look after in case the house went to pieces.

Before midnight the worst was over. When the men were sure the basement water was no longer rising but was falling, there was much praying, hymn singing and rejoicing, in which all joined. The maximum water height was 8 feet above the ground and only 6 inches below the floor.

By daylight the wind was down and the lightning, thunder, and rain were gone. None knew how our neighbors and their houses had fared. I remember being out on the back porch when the men pointed out three drowned persons in our backyard. They talked about the many nearby houses which had disappeared or were broken to pieces.

Mrs. Alma Walker, a cousin, and her husband, Frank, came to Grandmother's for the birthday party, spent the night, and all he found left at the site of their house was a hatchet![42]

The hurricane winds that came from the north brought silt out of Galveston Bay which covered the island. My recollection is that over one foot of the black slimy mud blanketed the surface all around us. Two white men (strangers on the island) were employed to clean our yard.

48. ". . . all he found left at the site of their house was a hatchet!"—Henry Cortes

They worked two days without finishing and never came back for any wages. It was thought they possibly became looters and were shot to death.

Fresh water for Galveston then came from wells at the mainland town of Alta Loma, as now. The water lines went down with the wagon bridge. Food became a problem. My father trudged through the mud to a grocery store and came back with a case of hardtack on his shoulder plus some boxes of oatmeal.[43] We were all glad to have anything to eat.

Each night we saw bonfires in a number of the directions where bodies were being burned. By day we saw horse-drawn express company wagons go by with bodies piled like cord wood. Some bodies were tied to weights, taken out to sea and dumped. Later, rumors were that some became loose and floated ashore. Anyhow, many people would not eat fish, shrimp, or crabs for several years.

Two or three days after September 8 we received word from a friend of my father, "Commodore" Bryan Heard (a cotton man of Houston) that he would come for us in his gasoline launch at an appointed time, and take us back to Houston. So at daylight on Wednesday, September 12, we crowded into a two-horse, old style hack, and by indirect routes we got through streets that were passable to the bay wharf.

Many strangers were camped at the wharves trying for the only way to get to the mainland. They cursed and threw things at us because they too could not leave the island. It was a small launch with room only for our family. After a long day's trip we landed at the foot of Main Street on Buffalo Bayou at Houston.

There is one blank in my memory. I don't remember any birthday festivities for my grandmother. My guess is that we kids had enough activity with the elements to keep us occupied.

It appears from what happened to others that what saved us and the Cortes house was:

1. The brick basement was built higher than a previously known hurricane['s] water had risen; it was well imbedded in the sandy ground; and it had sufficient arched openings for water passage.

2. The strong boarding inside and outside of windows and doors; and possibly the circumstance that my uncle was a druggist and had nearly a carload of mineral water which was used as support.

HARRY I. MAXSON

Harry Maxson, born in 1885, was the son of Willis and Isadora Maxson. His father, a prominent man in the railroad, brought the family to Galveston in 1897 when he became the superintendent of Santa Fe terminals. At the time of the storm, Harry lived with his parents, younger brother and sister near 40th and Avenue M½. This account surfaced among his personal papers after his death in April, 1967.

My family has asked me to write my experiences of the Galveston storm of September 8, 1900. At that time I was nearly fifteen and weighed 160 pounds and was full of excess energy. During school term I walked a mile and half to and from Ball High school, played run-sheep-run every chance I got. During vacation to keep me occupied and out of trouble, my father got me a job trucking freight in the Santa Fe Railway freight depot. My pay was 16 [cents] per hour. As we lived about 22 blocks southwest on 40th and Avenue M, and the freight depot was on 30th Street, I rode the street car back and forth to work.

The day of the seventh of September it rained steadily and through the night.[44] By noon of the eighth it was coming down in sheets and the wind had accelerated to gale proportions blowing from the north and northeast. About 10:00 A.M., the street cars had stopped running because of water over the tracks. By noon, telephones and lights were out and all business at a standstill. We kept on working under the greatest of difficulties until four o'clock when we were told to go home.

I had to wade in the middle of the street, and chose the middle as the wind was then blowing a hurricane and trees, signs, and roofs were being blown down. When I reached Avenue H, which was paved and had only about 2 inches of water in the center, I began to run as fast as I could. Running west on Avenue H about 35th Street, I got two shocks that made me wonder what was going to happen. I saw a roof being lifted off of a house. Believe me I sprinted as fast as I could as some shingles came toward me. I threw up my hand to guard my head and a nail in one of the shingles struck me and cut the back of my hand. At that minute—the wind, the water—dodging the shingles, I finally slipped and fell. I got some water in my mouth and it was not fresh, but salty. This was a jolt. How could salt water be in the center of the island which was three feet above sea level. I figured it must be from Galveston Bay. The wind was blowing so strongly from the North and Northeast had blown this bay water over the island. The water was about a foot deep by the time I got home—say 4:30 or 5:00 p.m.

Before going into the house I did my much disliked evening chore—milked Bossy and turned her out. She was the meanest cow that ever lived—would kick me and switch her tail in my face as if I were the fly that was biting her. I remember leaving the hundred foot rope on her halter, figuring that if she had to be rounded up in the morning I could catch her much easier with a rope attached to her. It was always impossible to throw a rope over her head as she always ducked out of its way most successfully. I couldn't feed the chickens and this was one of my chores, but one I liked, because the water was at least six inches deep in the chicken house and yard and all the chickens were up on the top roosts.

Upon entering the house I was surprised to find it full of our neighbors—some friends and some strangers. Mother in her usual thoughtful way had opened our house to anyone who wanted to come in. Before the storm was over we had about a hundred people in our house—men, women, and children, and Mother was constantly moving among them offering all the help and comfort she could. Our house was the largest and best built in the neighborhood. It had been built by the British Counselor and evidently he wanted it storm-proof.[45] First, the lot was raised two feet higher than the street and surrounding lots; the house of two stories was very strongly built on brick piers to the second floor. It had four fireplaces and a brick chimney in the kitchen. It was as if huge nails had been driven through the house from top to bottom. The first floor was a large basement and the seven rooms, two baths, hall and large front porch were on second floor. Most cottages and lots of two story houses without fireplaces floated away as soon as the water reached the second-floor.

Mother kept worrying about her young neighbor next door who was due to have a baby. The young couple lived in a small cottage that mother felt could not survive the storm. As soon as the water got high enough to get into their cottage, mother sent me over to tell the young couple to come over to our house. When I arrived there I found the stork had just delivered a baby boy. I returned home to get a ladder that some of the men and myself used as a stretcher for the mother. The water at that time was about a waist high in her cottage, and the wind was getting terrific. It was with the greatest of difficulty that we moved her into our house and a comparatively safe bed. The wind by this time had turned from the northeast to the east and was doing a lot of damage. Cisterns, fences, roofs, trees, et cetera were floating by. Every time there came a lull in the wind you could hear all kinds of queer and unpleasant noises.

Shortly after getting the mother and new baby settled, father showed up. I remember his new rain coat was torn to shreds from the wind. Father arrived about 9:00 P.M. The water was rising rapidly. We had been very concerned about father's safety and were greatly relieved when he appeared. By this time the wind was blowing much harder. The strongest gusts seem to last about two minutes and the lulls in between about five. However, the Weather Bureau reported the wind blew strong ½ minute and then let up one minute. The wind indicator broke at 100 miles per hour at about eleven o'clock, but the Weather Bureau estimated the wind got up to about 125 miles an hour about midnight.

Father anticipated what would happen to the house if the water got above the second floor level. It would float off. If one opened the doors or windows, which had strong green shutters, the next gust would lift the roof off and the walls would fall in. So, he asked me to get men to cut holes in the floor of each room. We had no tools in the house, so we used pocket knives and butcher knives. An almost impossible task to cut a three inch square in oak wood floors and under flooring. But we weren't going anywhere and we were glad to have something to keep us busy. The house was so full and there was so much worry and distress among the occupants that mother was kept busy making coffee, et cetera.

Each family was huddled together in corners under tables, so if the house went down they could all hang together. Father was busy holding the double stained glass front doors from blowing in. He had the largest Negro man I ever saw holding one of the doors and he the other as the wind would almost blow the door open. We took a table leaf out of the dining-room table and made it act as a brace under the front door handle and large nails driven in the floor helped a lot.

Every few minutes some woman would become hysterical and mother would comfort her. It seemed the home could not stand one more terrific gust of wind as it would rattle and weave like a duck blind in a storm. Often flying timbers, slate from roofs would hit the house like a cannon ball. There were plenty of people praying on their knees silently and out loud.

About 12:30 A.M. we heard a kid's voice between the blows yelling, "Please let me in—please let me in," which we did between lulls in the hurricane and will give you all the details in the concluding paragraph of this memo. About 1:00 A.M., father asked me to listen from one of the kitchen windows during lulls, and after getting all the people out of the kitchen I raised one of the windows about two [inches] and on my knees listened. I heard what I didn't want to hear, a woman yelling, "For God sake come and save us, our home is falling to pieces." I shut the window as quickly as I could and tried to forget that woman's voice. It was awful so far away and still so penetrating; it made me shake all over. I hoped it wasn't so—something fooling me, yet I couldn't run away. So after the next gust I opened the window again and sure enough the same call for help and she yelled, "I can see the lights in your house." I shut the window quickly and still on my knees prayed for help for them.

Something had to be done and as I was a very poor swimmer, but knew how to ride the waves and stay on my feet after a breaker passed over me, I decided to try to get some good swimmers to go out and rescue her. The first one I picked from the dining room wouldn't believe his own ears. After I took him to the kitchen and let him hear her yell for help—he said no, because he had a wife and two kids. The next one had the same excuse. Then I picked a big young truck driver who lived near us and had been married about a month. He had the same reaction I had when I raised the window. He didn't want to hear her. He listened again and said he'd go with me after he told his new wife goodbye. I told father what we had heard and that Bill was going with me, but I couldn't tell mother goodbye.

I took a broom out of the kitchen to feel my way in the water. As Bill and I opened the kitchen door and started down the back stairs we found a big horse standing at the corner of the stairs and we eased ourselves by him and started out for the house about a block west of ours. We could ride the waves and got about halfway there when I found a telephone pole which was a life saver for me to hang onto. Bill would guide it west and I would push from the other end. When I came to, Bill had me on the pole and explained a wire attached to the pole had flipped it back and we would have to give it up.

Our house was the last house that withstood the storm to the west and the block of homes west of us had been swept away. There was an old railroad track running north and south on 41st Street which was high enough to stand on and ride the waves. The house from which the woman was yelling had been floating for several blocks and as the wind had shifted to the southwest had landed it on the railroad tracks. Each gust would wash off part of the house. It lasted about an hour before it crumbled away.

When we got within about fifty feet of the house we could talk to the woman who had gotten out on top of the roof with several others. She told us they had 13 babies and children in the attic and there were 23 adults. I asked how many men—she said 10. Then I told her [we] would take the kids [on the] first trip and come back for the others later, but I wanted all the men to help us by carrying one kid each. Bill could carry two, he was a wonderful swimmer. The longest silence I ever heard, but no one came out or even said, "boo."

Another gust took off a part of the house and as I was yelling for the men to come out to the railroad track so we could tell them our plans, a short woman not tall enough to reach the railroad track rails pushed a baby in my arms and said, "Save my baby and let me go." She grabbed me around the neck and gave me a good ducking. I gave her to Bill and held the baby above my head. Then I realized the men in the house were paralyzed with fear, or just scared to death and there was no more use begging them to come out and help us.

So I threatened them by telling them we would save the two we had in our arms and let the rest go if they didn't come out. Not a word in reply, but almost immediately a large Negro man appeared with a white baby and I thanked him loud enough for all to hear and here they came—all the men with a baby each and some of their wives. We started back to our home single file holding on to the one in front of us, chain gang, and we had to take them north on 41st Street and Avenue N, then along the street car tracks to 40th Street, then south on street car tracks back to our house. This was much safer, as we could ride the waves and not have to swim all the way which would have been impossible.

By the time we squeezed our party by the horse on the back steps, Bill's wife had told mother where we had gone and she had a lamp in the kitchen cooking coffee and hot biscuits, which she kept cooking for 12 hours.

Immediately we started back with several men to help and cut across the block west of our house to the crumbling house on the railroad tracks and had no trouble detouring the balance of the 36 [people] on the tracks back to our house. This must have been about 1:30 A.M., and the gusts were less violent and the lulls were longer. A cyclone is all over when it passes, but a hurricane keeps blowing itself out gradually. By Sunday morning the sun was shining, but the water was still three feet deep in the streets and what a wreck it left.

Houses split half in two, others gone entirely and cisterns everywhere with all kinds of furniture, bales of cotton and most everything floating around. In all the excitement it's a pity we didn't get the names of all the people who were saved in our house that night, but the next few days in trying to count a total—so many in the parlor, dining room, under the tables, etc., bedrooms and the boy, Forrest Runge we let in the front door at midnight saying he floated on a rock, and the 36 from the house on 41st Street (it was all washed away by sun up) there was a minimum of 140 to a maximum of 150 people, not counting their pets, several dogs, cats and birds.[46]

Fortunately, our large cistern stood the storm, but mother's ample supply of groceries, coffee, bacon and flour was melting away mighty fast with so many mouths to feed. I was most happy to see our barn [and] chicken house were gone and with them my pet "Bossy," and I didn't look very hard when mother asked me to look for her for milk for the kids.

When I returned (delighted), father had written a note to Chief Police Ed Ketchum telling him how many we had to feed and to send mother some food. I made the best time I could getting to the City Hall. I remember seeing a Negro man shot for having a flour sack filled with mostly jewelry taken from dead bodies that were floating around everywhere.

Chief Ketchum told me how glad he was that father and family were O.K. He handed me a 45 Colts and a box of shells and a badge for he wanted to deputize father as an officer. Then he wrote a note to Fowler, Wilke, & Lang Wholesale Grocery Co. for our food and told me to hurry over there.[47] They were wonderful—commandeered the first 2-wheel dray that came along and started loading it with 3 sacks of potatoes, 3 sacks of flour, ten-gallon can of lard and filled it full with all kinds of food, especially canned salmon. (For ten days we had to eat canned salmon and I haven't wanted any since.)

It was about noon before we arrived home, but such a welcome I never saw. Some had had no food in 24 hours and there were plenty of hands to help peel potatoes and cook. After getting something to eat I had to go cruising to find some of my friends. I found some of them, but many of them I did not. One girl in our class was drowned in a cistern. How? You'd meet friends and you could tell without asking if all their family were O.K., or some missing. All you could say, "I am so glad, or so sorry," and go on looking.

About 35th and Avenue P. or Q, I saw a lot of men starting small fires and before I knew what had happened I had been conscripted to help bury or burn the dead. It was too gruesome to describe the condition some of these bodies were in. In less than an hour I looked up and saw Col. McCaleb, an officer of the Local Militia.[48] He said, "Harry, you're big enough, but too young to be doing this kind of a job." He wrote me out a pass and told me to go home which I was awfully glad to do.

I got home about 6:00 P.M. and by this time the water had drained off

49. ". . . I had been conscripted to help bury or burn the dead. It was too gruesome to describe."—Harry I. Maxson

the streets and most lots, but I found a woman corpse on the corner across the street and two boys, twins about five years old in the alley holding on to each other with a death grip. I got a shovel and buried them together in one shallow grave. Then I went to bury the woman, who had a small diamond engagement and wedding ring on and small diamond earrings. There was a lone man sitting on the curb by her with a bottle of whiskey, not drunk, but just sipping enough to keep him going, said he had been looking for his wife all day—could not get home last night and their place had been washed away.

I tried to get him to go on, but he wanted to stay and help me lay her away. I knew what he was thinking about—he just kept mumbling her name. After getting the grave dug large enough, I found a corrugated washing board and he helped me lay her in her grave so tenderly. It was pitiful! I put the washboard on her face and refilled the grave. Then he thanked me and walked south toward the gulf. I never saw him again.

Due to the excessive September sunshine and humidity there was nothing else to do but to bury those you could and those too decomposed burn their bodies which was worse. The closest estimate was 10,000 lost—identification was impossible.

Father really did a job that was a world's record and won him a gold watch of appreciation of the Citizens of Galveston and a 30-day vacation from the Santa Fe Railway, reestablishing rail communication with the mainland in 15 days.

There were 4 bridges washed away by the storm, Hiway, Sou. Pac. & GHH by Katy & IGN & the Santa Fe.[49] For 15 days and nights father never came home. I would take him food and clean clothes every night at midnight to a Pullman car where he slept and stay there to wake him at 4:00 A.M. Once I thought he needed an extra hour sleep and that was the only time he ever swore at me for not waking him on time.

What he did was to get two crews of men working 12 hours each, one day time that would lay the track using the ties and rail that the night crew had taken up from switch tracks in the railroad yards. Within three days he had the Santa Fe track to the bridge, and the other railroads gave up and rented the Santa Fe's. The pile drivers were working night and day from the Island as well as from the Mainland completing five miles of bridge within 15 days.

The second day I took father his gun and badge and he said, "Let's walk out to the Bay Bridge," so he could estimate the damage done and

50. ". . . I went to bury the woman. . . . There was a lone man sitting on the curb by her."—Harry I. Maxson

materials needed to repair the railroad. It was about four miles from Galveston and before we had walked a mile we noticed men running ahead of us and then they would take to the grass and hide until we passed. We soon found out what they were doing—stealing jewelry off the many dead bodies that had floated along until stopped by the railroad elevated tracks.

We passed several bodies, women in the majority and noticed they still had their earrings and finger rings on for about one mile. Then we noticed that all had been robbed from there on to the bridge. They had the ring fingers cut off and earrings pulled out of their ears and usually rolled over face down—no doubt looking for money. It was a gruesome sight never to be forgotten. When we returned, father reported it to Mr. Ketchum and he told us his department shot several of the ghouls the next day.

There were so many freak things that the storm did, it would be impossible to mention only a small part of what we saw the next day. However, just one to give you an idea of how much force and destruction a

51. ". . . two crews of men working 12 hours each, . . . that would lay the track."
—Harry I. Maxson

hurricane can do. Most of the damage was done by the wind coming from the East and SE and the fireplace in the SE bedroom was a large one. It rested on a brick foundation and was about five feet wide, two feet thick and possibly 25 feet high. A 2x10x40 had been shot like an arrow through the center of this brick foundation knocking a hole about a foot in diameter and knocked down one solid brick pier west of the foundation and the end was stopped by the next pier west, but the rear end of this timber was still sticking out of the foundation about two feet below the second floor of the house and about eight feet above the ground. We were all thankful that it did not tear through the house instead of the basement.

My friend, Mayer, was sitting with his mother half-way up the stairs in their large 2-story house one block east of us.[50] His sister was in a bed in one of the north bedrooms. During the storm the house was split in two, the north half melting away into the water and the stairs hung onto the south half which stood the storm. They never saw their sister again.

Due to the scarcity of food, water, et cetera, father thought best to get us out of Galveston on the first boat to Houston to the Mainland, which was in about ten days. We visited our many cousins, Andersons and Murrays at Putnam, Illinois for a month; then we returned to Galveston and found the Red Cross had things pretty well clean.

Many of my friends on hearing I passed through the Big 1900 Galveston Storm wanted to hear all about the details—and it was such a long sad story, I made a habit of telling it only once a year and that, of course, would be on Thanksgiving Day.

GENEVA DIBRELL SCHOLES

Geneva Dibrell Scholes, born in October, 1879, was the daughter of James W. and Marsaline Dibrell. She married Robert Scholes in 1898 and at the time of the storm they had one son, Robert Dibrell Scholes, for whom Galveston's airport is named today. She wrote this memoir of the storm for her second son,

52. "My friend, Mayer, was sitting with his mother half-way up the stairs. . . . the house was split in two, the north half melting away into the water and the stairs hung onto the south half which stood the storm."—Harry I. Maxson

Charles D. Scholes, born in 1903. Geneva Scholes passed away in Austin in 1968 at the age of ninety. Her account is a bit choppy, as she goes from one event to another without a clear direction.

DECEMBER 25, 1960

Dear Charlie:

Perhaps you might some day casually think I wonder what experiences my father, mother, and older brother, my maternal grandmother and my mother's little sister who were living in Galveston, had that terrible day.[51] So! Since time is hanging heavy on my hands I am going to tell you.

The Almanac of 1900 said very plainly we were due for a bad tropical storm. How many ordinary people give such reading matter more than a glance and forget all about it? We did just that until the night before the storm, when the wind was blowing a little stronger than usual; then your father reminded me of it.

Your father was Supt. of the Bridge and Building Dept. of the Galveston, Houston & Henderson R.R. Co. with headquarters at Virginia Point. When next morning he arrived at the depot he considered the waters of the bay were alarmingly high and turbulent; he hurried back home to try to persuade me to come to League City on the next train and stay there until the storm blew over; since his crew of B. & B. [bridge and building] men were working there painting the bandstand in the "Little Town Park".[52]

I assured him I felt no apprehension, since I was familiar with equinoctial disturbances; in fact, I tried to tease him, by saying he being from the north would eventually get used to our "Big Blows." He hurried back to the depot, caught the train, joined his crew and started the days work. By quitting time or even before, all wires were down and no information was available from Galveston.

Your aunt Marsaline and her husband and Uncle Charlie Dibrell were living in Dickinson; Victor Holland was depot agent and Charlie was studying telegraphy under him.[53] Your father and part of the crew spent the night of the storm in the present depot in League City. Early next morning your father, Alec M. Wright (Philipp's father), [and] the Roadmaster Mr. Corrigan started to make their way to Virginia Point. Corrigan couldn't swim, so he remained in Dickinson until the next day.

Dad and Alec Wright swam Dickinson Bayou and walked to Virginia Point where Alec located his wife, who had spent the night sitting with others on top of a freight "boxcar". She was holding one little boy and some man was holding the other boy.[54] As hours passed and the wind grew stronger both boys were lost.

There was no sign of any way to get from the Point to Galveston so Dad walked back to Dickinson and spent Sunday night with Aunt Marsaline and Victor and C.G.D. [Charles G. Dibrell] Early Monday he again started for Virginia Point, about noon a "relief train" from Houston arrived, Corrigan was aboard; about two o'clock that afternoon several little sail boats came from Galveston. The first one was swamped by a mob of sight-seers. One boatman called out, "If you have relatives on

53. ". . . Alec located his wife, who had spent the night sitting with others on top of a freight 'boxcar'."—Geneva Dibrell Scholes

the island, can swim to the boat and have twenty-seven dollars come aboard."

Dad had the seven dollars, the relatives and was a strong swimmer; Corrigan couldn't swim, so he gave Dad the twenty with the agreement to check on Mrs. Corrigan as soon as he found us; if Mrs. C. was safe (which she was, so was "Wrong Way" he was just a baby at that time) he was to come to the end of the island and wave his shirt, if she had been lost he was to come back and *not to wave.*[55]

As soon as the boat was loaded and under way the boatman said the fare was $7.00. Just about two hours before Dad reached home Monday afternoon, my Mother's oldest sister, Aunt Annie, who was living in Chicago, but a few days before the storm had come to Galveston to attend to business matters. She told the attendant at the hospital she had a sister living in Galveston; as soon as they had done all that could be done for her, she was placed on a dray and brought to us to care for.

She told us the house she was in [at] 17th and Avenue O had blown to pieces at about 4 o'clock Saturday afternoon. She clung to a part of the roof (she was a frail little old lady 75 years old). She recovered from her injuries, including a fractured skull; returned to her home in Chicago and lived a most active life until a few days before her death at 91 years. (Which strengthens my belief, one lives their allotted time.)

To continue, we had just finished making Aunt Annie MacAshen as comfortable as we could, when in walked Dad white and haggard, bare footed and almost exhausted, hadn't eaten anything since noon Saturday, but with a smile and encouraging words. As soon as he had a little food, he located Mrs. Corrigan and walked back to where he was to signal Corrigan; it was nearly dark when he again reached home.

Tuesday morning he worked getting our house as habitable as possible, Grandma and Aunt Frances came to our home because the cistern there did not overturn and was full of clean water and the underground cistern at Grandmother's home was of course contaminated. Her home was practically undamaged while our place was badly damaged, yet we chose ours because of the water, it is needless to say we had a hectic time to conserve it; we gave freely to people who came from blocks away with reasonable sized containers and requested them to use it *only for drinking* and to return for more when needed, which they did; but as soon as it became known we had water to share we were harassed by people bringing tubs of muddy clothing and wanting to use our precious drinking

54. ". . . our place was badly damaged."—Geneva Dibrell Scholes

water to wash the clothes; a colored man who rented a tenant house in the alley; whom I had allowed to bring his wife and two friends into our house during the storm, repaid me many times over by helping me to guard our cistern.

Tank cars brought in water two days later. If you recall, Charlie, the same condition existed after the 1915 storm when we lived at 29th and Avenue O.[56] When we had to almost fight those second hand merchants from West Market who insisted upon washing bolts of cloth they claimed to have bought and would not leave until you threatened to call the police; well as bad as conditions were in 1915—they were mild compared to 1900. It seemed like Fate for us to move from Galveston to League City three months after the 1900 Storm and move back to Galveston four days before the 1915 Storm.

Wednesday morning Dad joined the other bridge gangs and all of them worked in shifts day and night for a week during which time we did not see him, but we knew he was safe and doing his duty where it was needed most so! Grandmother and I did not feel neglected or abused when we had to guard the water; besides we had efficient help, believe me, as awful as things were Grandison and I had several good laughs when I couldn't convince some people I meant what I said; the minute I shrieked Grandison![57] It was funny to see how agile they became when that huge Negro came tearing out of his house, if they had already taken a little water it was usually spilled and Grandison would shake his fist and yell, "Next time a lady tells you to mind what she says, don't wait for the Lord to make you do it."

Just before dark Grandmother saw a man floating and struggling to get from the street in front of our house to a good sized live oak tree [that] had been blown over in the front yard; she thought that by some miracle Dad had gotten back to the island from League City and was trying to get to the house, we had a rope, so she tied it around my waist and I climbed through the branches until I could reach his hand, with the efforts of the three of us we made it into the house; as soon as I reached him I knew it wasn't Dad.

Our "Prize" was a Mr. Fisher, who lived four blocks from us (we did not know him) and he was gloriously drunk, first he wanted to know where the bar was, when I told him there wasn't any, he told me what he thought of that kind of a joint. Next he wanted a few matches, he was told we didn't have any, he looked at me in utter disgust when he saw I was crying, shook me and said, "Cheer up this wind will change at midnight." It really did *change* at about, but blew just as hard as it did the first way.

We had made as much preparation as we could by getting a ladder in so we could get in the attic if we thought it best, cut a big hole in each room floor, raised all the windows and opened the outside doors, blocked one front door with the piano, the other one with a dresser, in hopes we could prevent smaller things from being washed out. In the meantime the guest in the hotel was making fun of us for being afraid. There are four rooms in the main house and three in the newer addition, as an ell.[58] We had moved into this house just two weeks before the storm and hadn't gotten fully straightened, one room we did not need so I had temporar[ily] placed two wool blankets, a quilt, a *huge* dictionary and the family bible on a shelf just under the trapdoor going into the attic of the ell. This set up was just about the most shaky place to put a lighted lamp.

When I told Grandison he could bring his family into my home he asked if he could stay in the ell. I warned him, though that was the newer part I did not think it the safest part; I knew later why he preferred the ell, he was afraid I wouldn't want him to bring his friends in. Before he went to the ell I cautioned him not to light a lamp, we had no electricity; he promised he would do as I told him.

Mother and Frances, Robbie and I went to the attic; just before we did a neighbor and his wife came over to see if we would join them to go to the brick water works building; when we refused they decided to stay with us; we went to the attic. Mr. and Mrs. Wagstaff and Fisher remained below, Fisher said he thought he would go home to see if his mother, 82 years old, was all right.[59] We had been in the attic only a short time when Mr. Fisher had delirium tremens, not a sound from the Wagstaffs, I saw the roof of the house raise straight up about a foot and settle down exactly where it belonged, when up it rose again. I decided I'd come down, so did the roof, it is still where it was before the storm; when Mama saw me come down she followed me. Robbie weighed over 30 lbs. and I weighed 90, believe it or not, I ran one arm through the straps of his overalls, clung to the ladder with the other hand and I'm sure I set some kind of a record getting to the floor. Mother and Frances right behind me.

There sat Mrs. Wagstaff on my dresser, her feet on the foot board of the bed and Mr. Wagstaff had put the pillows under her feet so they (the feet) wouldn't get wet, because he was afraid she would take cold. He could find no trace of Mr. F. so presumed he had drowned, the water was between 5 and 6 feet deep around our house.

Tuesday morning while Dad was working to get the house ready to come back to it, a man passed by, he asked if he lived there when he was told he did, he said, my name is Fisher, your wife and her Mother saved my life; are they safe? I left their house in the middle of the night to go to my mother. Dad asked, "Did you find her?" Yes, she was hanging up on the headboard of her bed when I got home; she is O.K.

During the height of the storm we heard frantic screams from the direction of the ell of the house and then a terrific jerk of the main house and then all was quiet. We felt the Negroes in the ell had drowned. At daylight Sunday, two neighbor men came to find out if we were safe and to help us to get over to Mother's home 2½ blocks away, the wind was still blowing *hard,* we needed their help.

Before leaving we checked on the Negroes in the ell, the screaming we heard was from them when the ell had torn away and the blocks on one side had caved under; as we made our way in, to my consternation, there sat a lamp, on top of the family bible; still burning; upon calling again and again finally a wooly head showed up in the trap door—I was so startled at seeing that lighted lamp where it was. I began telling Grandison what I thought of him; his only reply was "We was skeered to stay up here cause rats might be up here." Indeed a strange choice—preferred a risk of burning to a rat's bite. To sum it up five Negroes scrambled out of that attic. It is still a mystery how they ever got up there.

When we got to Mother's home where the flood water was the same as where we lived and no preparation had been made, Mother had come over expecting the baby and me to come back with her; but found the wind so strong, advised we stay indoors, when she returned Sunday we were astonished to find aside from slime and mud on the downstairs floor, that everything was as she had left it, except a large dresser had turned over on its back and a lamp was laying over in the middle of the mirror—not even chairs or small pieces of furniture misplaced. The trap-door cap on the roof had been blown away—the sum total damage.

Some queer quirks were common. I had my dining room and kitchen in the ell of my home. On a narrow shelf of a side-board were six cut-glass glasses; not one slid off when the ell tilted, but a dinner set in the lower part of the side board was broken into fragments, just two whole pieces left–1 cup and a covered vegetable dish.

We continued to live in Galveston until November the 20th, 1900 when we bought a home in League City where you were born in 1903. In January 1904 Dad planted a live oak tree in our backyard so you two boys would have a shady place to play. That huge tree and the house where you were born will soon be only a memory, a sacrifice to progress. The Baptist Church interests have purchased the property. We can still cherish "Our Memories." Can't we?

Love, Mother.

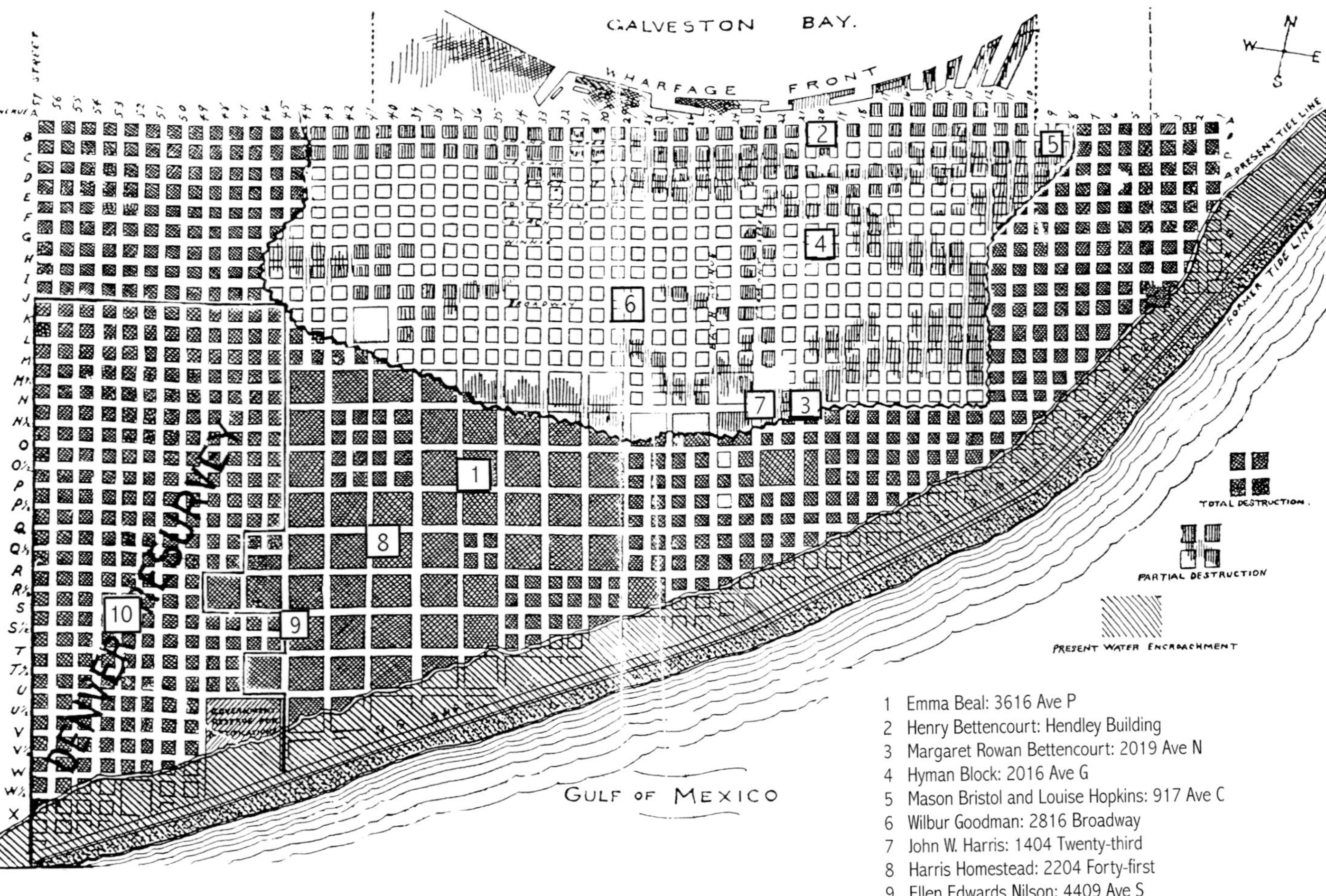
GALVESTON BAY.
WHARFAGE FRONT
PRESENT TIDE LINE
FORMER TIDE LINE
TOTAL DESTRUCTION.
PARTIAL DESTRUCTION
PRESENT WATER ENCROACHMENT
GULF OF MEXICO
DENVER RESURVEY
1 Emma Beal: 3616 Ave P
2 Henry Bettencourt: Hendley Building
3 Margaret Rowan Bettencourt: 2019 Ave N
4 Hyman Block: 2016 Ave G
5 Mason Bristol and Louise Hopkins: 917 Ave C
6 Wilbur Goodman: 2816 Broadway
7 John W. Harris: 1404 Twenty-third
8 Harris Homestead: 2204 Forty-first
9 Ellen Edwards Nilson: 4409 Ave S
10 Katherine Vedder Pauls: 53rd and Ave S

Survivor Oral Histories

EMMA BEAL

Emma Bernie Beal (1881–1972) was the youngest daughter of Emily Peale Chappell and Crawford Montgomery Beal. Her father worked as a dairyman and served three two-year terms as the Galveston county commissioner for Precinct 3 from 1882 to 1888. After his sudden death in 1898, the family moved into a newly built residence at 3616 Avenue P.

From 1906 to 1916, Miss Beal taught English at Ball High School. When her brother-in-law, Edward Goff, died in 1916 she took over his successful insurance company selling Aetna Life and Casualty Insurance.

Emma Beal gave two oral interviews to Marilee Neale for the Rosenberg Library in April and June, 1972.

The house wasn't high, but it was new. It was built in June and in September the storm came. I don't remember the water rising. I know my brother got the axe and he made a big hole in the floor so the water could come in.[1] People were coming in here to get out of the water and were scared to death. The water was so deep. We were all huddled in here and trying to be safe and dry.

The Tucker trees had people hanging in them.[2] Some of them were saved and some of them were not. The people who were saved held onto those trees. Any number of them got over here. The storm was over at midnight and the full moon came out just as pretty. There wasn't anything left. It was a clear space, except that old Tucker place. Now those

55. Emma Bernie Beal, 1899

little houses have been built since. That was all open space clear to the Gulf.

Mr. Cannon down the street was a commission man.[3] He'd send the provisions and my mother would cook for all the crowd. Men working on the street came in for coffee and stuff. She said, "Don't talk about my working; if I didn't have the work, I'd be crazy."

They had sent the bodies out in the bay, put weights on them and took them out, but they all floated back. So when they tried to bury some of them, there were so many they just went ahead and burned them.

I stood out there and watched them burn some bodies. It was right up across the street, on that corner of Thirty-seventh and P. I know one body, the arm went up like that, and I screamed. I never will forget that. I just saw the hand go up. I'd stand out there and watch them burn the bodies and then I'd have nightmares and scream and holler. Oh, it was a terrible thing. Something crazy about you when you watch anything like that.

HENRY BETTENCOURT

Henry Bettencourt was born in Galveston on December 4, 1891. During the summer of 1900, he and his mother, Henrietta Oppenbrink Bettencourt, were employed as laborers to pick strawberries in League City. As the strawberry season came to an end, Henry and his mother returned to Galveston.

In 1913, Henry Bettencourt married Margaret Catherine Rowan, whose account appears following his. They were the parents of four children. Mr. Bettencourt gave this oral interview to Marilee Neale in August, 1972, before his death later that year on December 18.

56. In his oral history interview, Henry Bettencourt claimed to be one of the young boys in the left of this picture.

We came to the Hendley Building on Twentieth and Strand [Avenue B].[4] My mother had a friend there that told her to stay there until she could be located somewhere else. We didn't know anything about a storm coming.

I saw all these horses coming down the Strand [Avenue B] moving west to higher ground. There was a wooden building across the street that had a restaurant downstairs, and it had one of these tin roofs that were pinched together.[5] At five o'clock that evening that roof rose up from both gutters, just like a hoop, and blew off. I was only two blocks from the City Hall, which had the fire department downstairs.[6] The third story was destroyed. We were only two blocks from the bay.

I was too small but all able-bodied men weren't allowed on the street unless they were put to work, cleaning up the city, moving bodies and all that. You see all the wreckage mostly in the southern part of the city, the Gulf side.

Sunday morning the sun was shining like nothing happened, but up on Twentieth Street from the bay up to Strand there was nothing but fishing boats. I never will forget it.

MARGARET ROWAN BETTENCOURT

Margaret Catherine Rowan (1890–1978) was the daughter of Kathleen "Kate" Wallstein and William F. Rowan. She was nine years old at the time of the storm and lived with her older brother, William J., older sister, Louisa, and two younger brothers, Hunter and Julius. Her father and older brother were employed as newspaper carriers for the Galveston Daily News.

Margaret worked as a night operator for Southwestern Bell Telephone Company until she married Henry J. Bettencourt on October 14, 1913. They raised one son and three daughters. One of their daughters, Dorothy Bettencourt Elfstrom, served as Texas' poet laureate.

We lived in a two-story house that was so high off the ground that a man could walk underneath at 2019 Avenue N. We weren't going to leave our home because my daddy said that the kitchen will be very strong because he had just built it. He said that would be the strongest. My daddy had a horse and he told my oldest brother to take the horse out, but the east wind was so strong. He had a raincoat and it went over his head. At that

57. "There was a store on the corner—Mr. Bader's butcher market—next door to our house."—Margaret Rowan Bettencourt

time they had cisterns and the horse came in between the house and the cistern and he wouldn't come out. The horse went on by himself and got saved by himself.

My daddy missed my brother and went out there and had to pull him out, that's how strong the wind was. He brought him in the house. The water was high. We had a little room we called the sitting room and it had a step up. We had a piano in that room and a piano stool, and the water was over that piano stool.

Then the boards off the front porch started breaking up. There was a store on the corner—Mr. Bader's butcher market—next door to our house.[7] The grocery store was down[stairs] and the people lived upstairs. Mr. Bader had to carry me on his back to get over to the store. They carried my sister and my brother and all of them.

We went over to the store and we went into the east room. My youngest brother was a baby then.[8] So my mother was holding my brother in her arms and the kitchen went down and a brick from the chimney blew off and hit that window and struck my brother on the temple.

These Jewish people lived on the other side of the grocery store, and they had a two-story house they lived in. When this two-story house moved out into the street, it hit the grocery store's back porch. I was asleep and my mother told me this part. The boys came into the room where the ladies were and said, "Mother, we want to tell you goodbye, all gone." And at that time the storm was over.

My mother said people were passing by, screaming and crying for help and had no clothes on. The wind had ripped all their clothes off. They'd been in the water and the water had gone down. They were trying to get help, for people to take them in and help them. We weren't allowed to go back in our house, because the mud was deep. They had to take shovels and shovel that mud out and they had to tear all the matting out. Oh, the odor was terrible! It took about two weeks before they'd let us go over there.

I had a grandmother and aunts and uncles who lived in the East End

58. Sacred Heart Catholic Church. "She got saved on Broadway at that church, Sacred Heart."—Margaret Rowan Bettencourt

and their houses were just splinters. My Grandmother Wallstein didn't want to leave her home.[9] Two uncles picked her up, put her in a boat and sailed her. She got saved on Broadway at that church, Sacred Heart.[10]

They never would've found her place, but my aunt had a "polly" [parrot] that was up in the attic and the attic didn't go to pieces. It just sat on top of the house and the next morning the Polly was hollering "Pretty Polly. Pretty Polly." That's how they found where they lived.

We left and went to Houston. My brother had a very weak stomach and couldn't stand to look at dead people. My daddy was a Knight of Pythias and they all got together and got their families and as soon as there was a train to leave out of here, they sent all their families to Houston.

They kept them there until they cleaned up here in Galveston for about a month. We couldn't wait to get home. We begged let us come home.

HYMAN BLOCK

Hyman Block, son of Leopold Block and Fannie Kahn, was born in Galveston on June 22, 1888. At the time of the 1900 storm he lived at 2016 Avenue G (Winnie) with his parents, older brother Henry, and younger sisters Gertrude, Rosa and Mamie. According to the 1900 census, the Block family also provided room and board for six boarders and employed two black servants.

Hyman Block went back to school in the fall of 1901. He later worked for a short time for the Hutchings-Sealy Bank. In 1904 he went to work for H. Kempner and Company and remained there until he retired in 1964. He enlisted in the U.S. Naval Reserve in 1917 and served as a cable (telegram) censor in the Western Union building at Twenty-first and Avenue B (Strand). He was involved in intercepting the infamous Zimmerman telegram, which helped fuel the mounting war fever in the United States and, coupled with the German decision to wage unrestricted U-boat warfare, resulted in America entering World War I.

Mr. Block received his religious training from Rabbi Henry Cohen and conducted services at Temple B'nai Israel in Rabbi Cohen's absence. He granted this interview to Robert Nesbitt in February, 1980. He died on July 19, 1982.

The night before was a Friday night on September seventh. As far as I can remember, it was a beautiful moonlit night. I seem to recall that our

59. Hyman Block in February, 1980, telling his story to Robert Nesbitt

entire family sat on our front porch and enjoyed the cool breezes. We had no inkling of a severe storm approaching. The stories are that they had a few notices, but they didn't have the intense communication that they have today. They did have Dr. Cline, who was the meteorologist, and he had no indication that it was going to come in this far.

I woke up about seven o'clock in the morning and it was cloudy and raining. It was blowing a little bit. I played around a bit and about eleven or twelve o'clock it commenced to blow a little better and everybody realized that we were going to have a good blow. There were three people who were in my home at that time, my father, brother and a very good friend, Mr. Miller.[11]

I was living at 2016 Winnie, right next to Saint Mary's Cathedral. My father went to work and we never saw him until the following morning. He worked at the Star Clothing House on Twenty-fourth and Market Street [Avenue D].[12]

My brother came home for his midday lunch. He was working at Miller Brothers.[13] At that time we had a garret at our house. In the summer you left the cover over the roof vent open so the air could come through. That thing was blowing around and I went up a ladder with my brother inside the house, who went out on the roof and he like to got blown off. He finally got that thing tied.

I still had no inkling what was going on. I guess our first realization of something bad was about four o'clock in the afternoon. We noticed lumber floating by and the people were then commencing to seek shelter at the courthouse. We could hear the cows mooing, dogs barking, the shouting and one thing and another.

About four-thirty it was raining pretty good and we looked out and right in front of our house was a man with horses. He was riding one and on the other was a lady with a very young baby. She was the wife of Clint Wolston and she was carrying Clint Wolston, Jr. who was only a year old. Clint's father was the county commissioner.[14] Realizing the danger to his family, who lived on Twentieth and Church [Avenue F], he sent his hack driver to get Mrs. Wolston and the baby. I don't know where they were going to take them.

As they came around on Twenty-third Street, the wind got them. A telephone pole fell across the hack and broke it in two. The man was fortunate enough to unhitch the horses and they put Mrs. Wolston and the baby on one horse and he on the other. When they got in front of our house and my mother saw them she went to the window and yelled out, "Bring those people in here!"

The sidewalk was about a foot off the street and the horses had to get over that. They came up to our porch and my mother reached out and almost fell in. My sister held onto her and she took Mrs. Wolston and the baby and brought them in. The man said, "What is your name?" and we told them. I didn't have any idea what was going on.

A couple of men came in about that time and asked if we knew what was going on and could they stay. They said, "Sure." "You never know what is going to happen," they said, "We might have to get out of this house." This was maybe five or six o'clock.

The water was then just about up to our front door level, which was about four or five feet off the sidewalk. He said, "I hate to tell you this, but we are going to have to chop a hole in your floor so your house doesn't float off." So they proceeded to pull up the carpet and chop holes in the living room and the dining room and the water came through.

We had a dining room table that my mother attempted to serve some food on. I remember it was some salmon and black coffee, and while we were sitting there eating, the table floated. We had about two or three feet of water inside the house, which was a total of six or seven feet of water.

They had noticed that this lumber was still floating around. They were about two-by-twelve boards which had been on a dredge which had been spilled by the storm. They floated about a half a dozen of them inside our house, because you never know when you are going to need something like this. We sweated out that storm, so when the water was getting that high, they took those same boards and put them up the stairway and they pushed the piano up the steps.

We got worried about where we were going to sleep. I think I slept a little and all of a sudden I heard a little noise and I found out the next day what had occurred. These men saw the water rising and about ten o'clock they went out on our upstairs front porch and they used those two-by-twelves as battering rams. It was about ten feet from the east end of our upstairs front porch to the window of Saint Mary's Cathedral school across. Using those planks as battering rams, they forced them over and they managed to get that window up into Saint Mary's. They fastened those planks so that we would have an escape if necessary.

Then I commenced to get scared to death. My mother was worried. Everything was being damaged. She was worried about my father. My brother wasn't home. My friend Mr. Miller wasn't home. I remember about four or four-thirty, the first one who got into the house was my father. He had a very narrow escape.

He and an uncle, Dan Kane, had been working at the Star Clothing House and by that time the storm had commenced to abate and they had waded through the water of the city streets, which was then approximately shoulder high.[15] They had to detour to come up Church Street [Avenue F]. Just as they got on Church Street, between Twenty-second and Twenty-first, a new brick building had just been built by E. Dulitz, a furniture store. That thing collapsed. They like to have got buried under those bricks.

On the morning of September ninth, we didn't know what had hit us. It was clear. We had been fortunate because Saint Mary's Cathedral shielded us and a building on the other side shielded us too. We got a whole lot of the blows from the front. An attic thing blew off and the whole upstairs was a mess.

You could hear people hollering. By nine or ten o'clock in the morning, people were flocking into the county court house for refuge. They

60. "By nine or ten o'clock in the morning, people were flocking into the county court house for refuge."—Hyman Block

were coming from the outlying parts. They were bringing their horses, their cows, and their children. They were mostly from down the island people. They made an awful lot of noise.

About five o'clock there was a knock on the back door. I think it was Bishop Gallagher.[16] He wanted to know from my mother, how was everybody. Then he came up with a fine idea. He said they had a cistern over at the parish house, where the priests lived. It had become contaminated and he wondered if we had tried any of the water in that upper cistern. We knew that our lower cistern was salty. We opened a tap and the water was fresh. He got some water to use for the holy water that they use and he also got authority to come and take all the drinking water they needed.

Monday morning I met Marion Levy and he said, "Hyman, they tell me there is a lot of people who have been hurt and they haven't got enough room for them over at the undertaking establishment. Let's go over and see it." The water had receded, but it was slimy and muddy and everything. We could see the damage.

In those days all of the express companies had these very high bins. They were about ten to fifteen feet high. They were built especially to carry loads of cotton samples. We saw four or five of those things stacked to the top with dead bodies and we got a breath of air and that is as far as I went.

My sister, Rose, had been on a visit up the state and she was trying to get back to Galveston. She got as far as Texas City and couldn't get in because they were not allowing anybody in or out of the city. She was fortunate enough to meet Mrs. Clara Barton. She told her story and said that she lived in Galveston and was anxious to get home to her family. Mrs. Clara Barton dressed my sister in a Red Cross uniform and they came by boat from Texas City to Galveston.[17]

Then the city caught its second breath. Order had commenced to develop out of chaos. The balance of the story you know what happened. The committees and so forth. Things began to stabilize to a certain extent. The federal troops were here and had taken over everything and established a commissary. About the third or fourth day, my brother was on his way to go to work at Miller Brothers and he was impressed in the service. He was made a deputy Marshal and given a bottle of whiskey and his job was at the Mensing Building.[18]

They were still continuing their efforts to identify bodies. As fast as they were bringing bodies in, they were bringing them into Mensing's and stacking them on the floor. He had to guard them because there had been a number of cases, and it was proven that people with rings on their fingers were losing them. Most of them were naked. There was a horrible stench. My brother stayed there about six days before they got him out of it.

They took these bodies and put them on barges and took them out to the ocean and the ocean brought them back to them. That's when they gave up and started burning all the debris wherever it was.

I remember the policing of the city. I was very much impressed by the United States soldiers that were establishing camps. They had camps right at my front door in the City Park. In the meantime, they took the

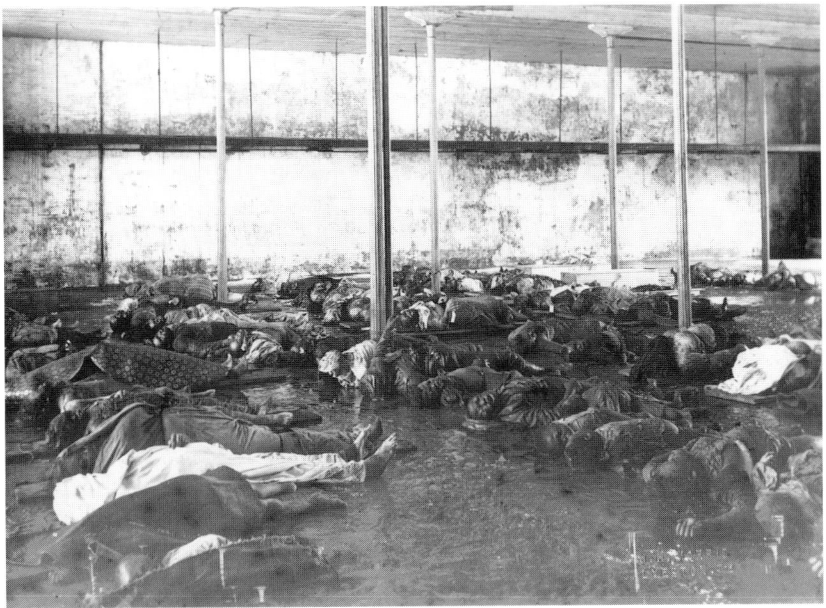

61. ". . . they were bringing them into Mensing's and stacking them on the floor."
—Hyman Block

federal troops out of Galveston and they brought in the Texas National Guard. They patrolled the streets. They would impress anybody who wasn't working. They didn't give a damn who you were. You had to go out and lift lumber and serve on [a] fire, and try to straighten things out.

One of the aftereffects of the storm was that for months we were unable to get rid of it. When the water receded, it left a silt behind it. As that dried out it stunk to high heaven. Everybody had the same problem. Many people lost their floor coverings. It was awful. We were on bare floors.

In about October of 1900, the people came out of the daze in Galveston and they started to rebuild. I remember distinctly that I stood on the corner and watched some roofers working on a building at the northeast corner of Twenty-first and Market [Avenue D].

WILLIAM MASON BRISTOL

William Mason Bristol, born January 19, 1879, was the son of William H. Bristol and Cassandra "Cassie" Stump. His father, an engineer, died in

62. U.S. soldier camps in City Park

December, 1893, and the family lived at 917 Avenue C (Mechanic). William and his older brother, John William Stump Bristol, supported the family, including two younger sisters, Lois and Mary Louise, by working as railroad clerks. Cassandra Bristol also took in medical students as boarders. After the 1900 storm, William Bristol continued working for the Southern Pacific Railroad for fifteen years. He later served more than twenty-five years as payroll auditor for the Affiliated National Hotel Company in Galveston.

Mr. Bristol gave two interviews to Marilee Neale in February and March, 1972. He died September 1, 1973.

We knew there was a storm coming, but we had no idea that it was bad as it was. We didn't have a Weather Bureau that gets it weeks ahead the way they do now. That's why there were so many drowned, so many lost. They didn't think it was gonna be as bad as it was and they stayed home. That whole part of the city banked up with all the debris.

I lived at 917 Mechanic and all but the back part of the house blew off. There was about four to five feet of water in the house. The water went down about eleven o'clock.[19]

Everything was over at eleven o'clock. I got out to walk. I was going to see a young lady—that I was supposed to have married—to see if she was all right. There was a deep gully that the tide had washed on Eighth Street. A deep gully down there. I went through down that gutter and uptown to see if she was all right. The hospital was on the other side of the gully.

As I stepped up on the other side, there were three bodies laying on the ground out there. I turned around and went back home. We had so

63. "I was very much impressed by the United States soldiers that were establishing camps. They had camps right at my front door in the City Park."—Hyman Block

much death here that the drays would drag out a dray load and put them on a barge and bring them out way out into the Gulf and dump them out there. They all floated back. They had to burn them out on the beach. After the storm was over, martial law started right up. It was quite a few people that they had to shoot for stealing. They had orders to shoot people they thought might get in and try to rob them.

I worked as a station accountant for the Southern Pacific Railroad during the storm. It had washed all the tracks off out in the West End. We had to have those repaired and we had to clear the right of way. We started pretty quick to try and get the right-of-way cleared so we could run the trains again.

We had a gang of men that'd go out there and clear away the debris that was out there. There were quite a few bodies laying out there in the grass. They were beginning to make a bad smell. They dug holes and dragged the bodies to them and put them in. One instance there were two or three sisters from the old orphans' home out here that were buried out there.

R. WILBUR GOODMAN

Robert Wilbur Goodman, born September 21, 1887, was the son of Henry B. and Maria Louise Goodman of Virginia. The Goodman family moved into their home at 2816 Broadway in 1895. At the time of the storm the family consisted of Wilbur, his parents, older brother Burleigh, younger sister Florence May and younger brother Lawrence. Also living in the house were a female schoolteacher who boarded there and two black servants.

After the storm, Goodman finished school and went to work in the bookkeeping department of Bell Telephone Company. He bought into the Model Laundry in 1910 and remained active in it until he sold his interest in 1970. He married Anna E. Butler and they had two children. He was active for more than sixty years in the Galveston Rotary Club and El Mina Shrine Temple and served on the school board, the Galveston Orphans Home board, and the Galveston Merchant's Association.

He granted this interview to Robert Nesbitt in January, 1975, four years before his death on February 18, 1979.

The storm was on September eighth. That was on a Saturday morning. I went to the YMCA that morning at Twenty-third and Winnie

[Avenue G]. I caught the last streetcar going home, the old Twenty-seventh streetcar. I got off at Twenty-seventh and Broadway and walked to the house. The wind was blowing and the rain was coming down, but the water hadn't yet come over the city.

After dinner [lunch] that day, my brother and I asked my father if we couldn't go out and see how the Gulf was acting. We went on down Broadway to Twenty-third Street until we got as far as Avenue P. The water wasn't quite waist deep, but it was too deep for us, so we decided that we wouldn't go any farther.

On the way back, we stopped at a man's house and the water then was just up to his porch, almost ready to come into the house. When we approached the house he said, "What are you boys doing out in weather like this?" We said, "We are trying to make it home now." He said, "You can't make it now. The wind is coming out of the northeast and hurricane winds are counterclockwise."

We couldn't walk. We had a walking stick, some kind of a stick we picked up. We tried to walk against that wind and we couldn't. He said, "You had better stay here tonight. I don't think you can go any further." We told him we couldn't do that. Our mother and father were expecting us. We looked out and saw a hack coming down Tremont Street.

It was about three or three-thirty in the afternoon. I told this brother of mine, who is three years older than I am, "Well, Burleigh, let's see if we can't hop a ride behind that hack." So we did. We ran out and as the hack passed we hopped on the big springs on the back of it. We rode that hack back to Broadway and then we walked to our home on 2816 Broadway. When we got home the water was up to our waist.

By that time the bay water was coming in from the bay. The bay and the Gulf waters were meeting, the tide had come up so high. When we entered the home, our mother and father were at the front door and they didn't know whether we would be able to make it or not. They were very glad to see us.

In about a half an hour, the water was over the fence. If we had waited, we never would have made it. The wind was picking up. In those days everyone had wooden blinds or shutters on their home. The wind was blowing them off. The slate [roof] was coming off that house. It sounded like a freight train passing over the roof of the house. The water was coming through the roof and we were staying on a lower floor.

We never realized what was going on south of us. The major damage was from Broadway south. The next morning, when we got up, we didn't realize what had taken place during the night. Mr. Russell, who was a friend of my father's, came up on the steps of the house and he was in wreckage.[20] Mr. Russell knocked on the door and my father said, "Mr. Russell, come on in. Why are you in the condition you are in?"

He said, "Mr. Goodman, you have no idea. There are thousands of people who have lost their lives here. I'm the only member of my family that was saved. The only reason that I am saved is that at my house the second floor separated from the first floor and I crawled up in the attic of our house and that section of our house floated on the debris of the other houses that had gone down. I stayed up in the attic until the water had subsided. Then I crawled off the debris and got back on the ground and here I am."

He lived out on [Avenue] O or N½ out that way. He said, "There is nothing standing south of Avenue N. Everything is gone. There is nothing." So we took Mr. Russell in and he took a bath. We had a large cistern and we furnished water for the whole neighborhood. We had no city water. The mains had been broken.

We had a high-raised house and when we thought the water was coming in the house we got a bit and drilled holes in the floor. [My father] didn't want to damage the floors, because they were all solid oak floors. We put a pencil down there and the end of the pencil was already wet by that water. He said, "If the water gets any higher, we are going to have to drill a lot more holes, because I want that water to come through those holes. I don't want it to do any more damage than necessary." The water got within three inches of that floor and that is as high as it got.

There was a Mrs. Thompson who worked at the old Clarke and Courts. She lived on west Broadway. She got as far as our house and she couldn't get any further. She came in and asked if she couldn't stay there. The water was just getting too deep and she couldn't go any further. She spent the night with us.

There was a young fellow that was in a tree, or a telegraph post, out on the esplanade. A good swimmer could swim from the other side of the street to our house, but he couldn't swim back. He went by that post and asked that young fellow if he could swim. He said, "No, I can't swim a lick." The swimmer said, "I'm sorry, but the wind is so strong and the water is so rough that I'm not going to be able to get you over to that house over there." He was pointing to our home. He swam and

64. Photo taken on top of wreckage showing city south of Avenue N. "There is nothing standing south of Avenue N. Everything is gone."—R. Wilbur Goodman

came right up on the porch of the house. We let him stay with us that night.

I said, "Well I don't think that young fellow will survive the storm." He said, "I don't think so either." Then about midnight, a full moon came out. For some reason or another, the skies began to clear and there was a full moon up there. As fate would have it, a big tree floated up and lodged against that telegraph pole and he stood on that tree and when the water went down he came over to our house.

The water began to go down pretty quickly. After the storm they set up dozens of commissary houses, that we used to call "shotgun" houses.[21]

JOHN W. HARRIS

John Woods Harris III, born on September 23, 1893, was the son of John Woods Harris, Jr., and Minnie Hutchings. At the time of the 1900 storm, his family, including his thirteen-year old sister Florence, and two servants, lived at 1404 Tremont (Twenty-third) Street. After the storm, Harris attended Galveston schools, and was graduated from Episcopal High School in Alexandria, Virginia. After enlisting as a second class seaman in 1917, he taught at the Navy Flying School in Pensacola, Florida. He then finished his law degree at the University of Virginia in 1920.

He returned to Galveston in 1920 to manage the Harris estate and became involved in many civic affairs, including the Rosenberg Library's board of directors and the Sealy and Smith Foundation. In 1930 he became director of the Hutchings-Sealy National Bank. Harris established the Galveston Foundation in 1973 to support the beautification of the city. Harris Garden, located on the corner of Twenty-third Street and Broadway, was dedicated in May, 1997, in honor of his parents.

This interview was conducted December 22, 1980, by Robert L. Jones. Mr. Harris died February 22, 1999, at the age of 105.

The storm was on the eighth of September and on the twenty-third, which was my birthday, I would have been seven. I remember seeing my father coming home in boots up to his thighs and waist and walking up that front walk. What an amazing sight that was.

The water was six feet deep on Tremont Street at that time. Our place had been raised about two feet above and the house was a brick house. The first floor was six feet above the gardens, which was about all that saved the house that night. The water just got to the level of the front door, which was eight feet above Tremont Street.

There were about twenty-four refugees I remember that came in through the front parlor. The parlor was on the front side of the entrance. They came through the windows there. I remember Mother served them all food around twelve o'clock, when the height of the storm was over and the water began to recede and the wind so that they could leave.

I remember we were all frightened. My sister and I were the only two children. The old yardman had brought a raft around to the kitchen and tied that up in case we had to abandon the house. Mother had a trunk

65. Residence of John W. Harris II. "Our place had been raised about two feet . . . and the house was a brick house."—John W. Harris III

strap around each one of us to hold onto us as long as she could. We had it around our waist at the height of the storm because some of the bricks blew out on the second story and you could see the lightning in the rain through the open south side of the house.

The old Harris homestead where my aunts and my cousins lived was completely destroyed.[22] I lost eleven relatives in the 1900 storm. I remember the mayor came in the next morning. He said to Father, "John, your whole family is destroyed." I remember that's the first time I ever saw Father with tears in his eyes. He had no idea the extent of the damage. We hadn't left the house yet. He said, "I'll get out there right away." I think it took him two or three hours walking over wreckage and things to get to the old home. There he found Aunt Lillie and Aunt Rebecca and their children. Eleven in all in the old home just completely collapsed and destroyed.

I was only seven. My father wouldn't let me get out because of the bodies and things around. So I stayed in. Our place went right through to Twenty-second Street and had about seven lots in it. They kept me inside the fences and I couldn't get out; I didn't know. I remember hearing that some man was impaled on the fence.

MARY LOUISE BRISTOL HOPKINS

Mary Louise Bristol Hopkins, the daughter of William H. Bristol and Cassandra "Cassie" Stump, was born July 11, 1893. Her father died when she was only five months old, leaving her mother, two older brothers, and an older sister. After William Bristol's death, Cassie Stump Bristol mortgaged their little cottage at 917 Avenue C (Mechanic) and enlarged the home to take in medical students as boarders. After the storm the family took on a second mortgage to rebuild the home and have it raised.

Louise Bristol left school while in the seventh grade and enrolled at Draughton's Business College. She took her first job at Flatto's Shoe Store and then worked for eleven years at the Santa Fe Railroad. She secretly married Oscar Hopkins in January, 1913, but they continued to live apart until her family learned of the union. The couple married again in February, 1914.

Mrs. Hopkins continued to be active throughout her life, devoting more than ten thousand volunteer hours to Saint Mary's Hospital and working with the Episcopal Church. She often spoke to schoolchildren in Houston and Galveston about her life and experiences during the 1900 storm. She gave this interview to Jane Kenamore in July, 1982, five years before her death on November 18, 1987.

I remember seeing the water come down the street and being so delighted that we didn't have far to go to the beach. It was right there at the front door and then it began to get bigger and wider and was coming into the garden that my mother had. That distressed me to think she had so little time for those things and then to have them ruined that way.

My sister was eight years older than I. My two brothers had left early that morning because they didn't anticipate anything like this. They both had jobs. They came home and helped my mother. I saw my brothers coming home. The older one was there early and the other one. I remember seeing him wading in water up to his chest, holding his arms out like this to walk against the wind and the water.[23] It frightened me.

We got as much as we could out of the cabinets. I even helped with the lighter things. When my mother realized that the water was going to come in the house, that it was coming under the door in the house, she went out to where she chopped kindling wood for the stove. She got an axe and chopped holes into every floor of every room downstairs in the hallway and the kitchen and the dining room. So the water would come up into the house and hold the house on the ground.

We all got upstairs and I looked out of the window and I could see that the water was over the baluster of the house next door.[24] I don't think I was frightened until then. I thought, if it's that deep in their house, how deep is it my house? I thought of all the things that had to be left behind—the beds, the heavy pieces of furniture.

My brother went in the room out over the kitchen and dining room. He said he didn't believe it was shaking as badly there as it was in the front part of the house, and that we should go out there to see. So we all held hands, because the wind was blowing just terribly and went across an open porch to back there. We were no sooner back there and my mother said, "It's worse out here than it was in the main part of the house." So we went back to the main part of the house.

Now she said we should have a light in case somebody was out in the storm and could see a light. They would know somebody was there and alive. You couldn't put a lamp on because the house was shaking so badly that we were afraid it would fall off and set the house on fire. There was no pan Crisco in those days. She bought lard in drums and my sister had a little carnival stick with a flag on the end of it. She put that across the top of the open can of lard. She took a piece of material she tore off of something and she saturated that down in this lard and [put it] on one end over the little stick and lighted that as a wick. That's the light we had through the night. That weird little light burning there.

All of a sudden, my sister screamed and pointed into the door into the room next door and that wall was leaving that ceiling. It was going out each time a gust of wind would come. It would go out and then come back in again. My mother was the only [one] that wasn't surprised. I feel like she had seen it before my sister did. She realized that the house was going to pieces around us. She knew that the back end had already gone off, because we heard the crash of that.

We had heard the crash and my mother went to the porch and looked out and saw everything she had worked for in the yard next door. She said—I remember her words so—"Oh God. Why couldn't we have all gone with it." It had been such a struggle to her up to that time and she just didn't see how she could face another.

So we were just waiting for the part we were in to go to pieces. We had to make some provisions to get out. We knew that the people across the street, the Dau family, was still there.[25] Their house was a high-raised house and they had a cow they kept under the house. They had a lantern and we knew that they were still there. It was such a consolation to know that somebody was still alive.

My mother said, "We'll try to make it over to the Dau's. They're still over there, just across the street." My brothers were good swimmers. My mother took the mattress off the bed and my sister and she and I were going to hold onto the mattress and my brothers were going to try and pull us. I don't know what she'd planned for us to do, but we were going to try to make it over.

Then she realized that the wind was blowing so terribly enough to do that damage that we were liable to be blown away. She took sheets off the bed and tied us to her. But as we watched this going out and coming back in again, my sister kept saying, "Wait." My mother would say, "Let's go now." My sister would say, "Wait." If we hadn't waited I'm sure we never would have made it across.

The storm began to go down and we saw Mr. Dau come out of his house with the lantern. We called to him and I remember my brother saying, "My God, you're not leaving us now!" He said, "I'm going down to see about my cow."

Anyway, we survived. I remember my mother saying, when she saw the house, "Here goes the mortgage." It was sad for her. She had a sad life and she was a very smart woman.

I wasn't permitted to leave the house. As soon as the water went down, my two brothers left to see about some relatives that lived not too far away. They were conscripted to help with the burying of the dead and getting people that were under the wreckage. They were told they must help and then they were told they had to dig. There was no identification and no prayers said or anything else, the bodies were just put in the ground. There were so many of them that they couldn't find any more ground to bury them. They took them out to sea and then they washed back in again, so they had to be burned.

It was a terrible time. I was saved all that, but I heard the stories of

66. ". . . my two brothers . . . were conscripted to help with the burying of the dead."—Mary Louise Bristol Hopkins

women with long hair who had been caught in the trees by their hair and cut to pieces with slates that had been flying off the roofs of houses.

I remember my mother. We went out to the porch to look at our house, because the back end of it had completely collapsed and it was in the yard next door. Everything, cook stove, the two bedrooms upstairs with all the furniture and all the dining room furniture and everything was in the yard next door.

I can remember crying the next day. We had plenty to eat, because she'd gotten all the food upstairs. But I was crying because it was raining in my beans and I couldn't stop it from raining. I remember a silly little thing like that.

Then came the commissary, you know people in the North sent things down, old clothes. They were new, but they were out of style. I remember my sister and I both got little suits. She didn't want to wear hers. I think mostly because I had one like it.

ELLEN EDWARDS NILSON

Ellen Edwards Nilson, youngest daughter of James and Charity Edwards, was born in Devonshire, England on October 10, 1880. Her parents brought their seven children to Galveston in 1883. James died there in 1884, and Charity worked to keep her children out of orphanages until her death in 1895.

At the time of the 1900 storm, Ellen lived with her older brother, James, and sister Eliza at 4409 Avenue S. She married Niels Nilson and they had two children. Her nephew, Johnny, survived the storm and resided in Houston. She gave this interview to Rev. Glen Echols of the Central Methodist Church at an unknown time before her death on February 16, 1966.

I remember the 1886 storm, so when the 1900 storm came I wasn't the least bit worried. The wind started to blow bad on Friday. It was the seventh of September and I thought we're having an early fall. We had a hard wind, but the sun was shining. My brother worked at night.[26] When he came home Saturday morning, he brought my sister Mary that lived on Eighth and L.[27] She had married and lived there and had two children.

When she came in I said, "Well, I'm surprised. I was thinking about you and if the wind had been in the other direction I would have been worried." She said, "You better start worrying. The water is waist deep in our yard now." That was Saturday morning, about eight o'clock. She had left her mother-in-law there and her mother-in-law was not self-sufficient. She wanted to go back and see about her. Also, she didn't have good enough clothes for the children.

She wanted to go back and Brother said, "This will be over in a few minutes. Don't worry about it. It'll be over in a little while." So I said to her, "Mary you wait until Jim goes to sleep and you can go back. Don't say any more about it." They were arguing about it. Mary and I went down to Eighth and L, leaving her two children with my sister Janey, who we all just called Sister. She and my sister, Eliza, were there. Sister had been sick and was sitting up for the first time that day. We left the children there and went back. When we got as far as Seventeenth and L, the [street]car wouldn't go any farther. It was too much water. So we got out and walked. The water was up to our knees.

When we got to the house, my brother-in-law was there and he had seen to his mother and all. We begged him to come back with us, but he

67. Murdoch's Bathhouse. "The bathhouse had already gone, but we didn't know that."—Ellen Edwards Nilson

wouldn't. He said he'd be out after a while. So we went back on the last car that went out to what then was Denver Resurvey, west of us. That was about eleven o'clock in the morning.

We got the children and went home. I went in and cooked dinner and still wasn't very worried. We ate, my brother and sisters and the children. We were there and all of a sudden my cousin came in and he said, "You all get out of here. The bay has backed up." Now he and my brother-in-law were out on the beach getting timbers. The bathhouse had already gone, but we didn't know that. They were pulling in some of the big timbers and looked behind them and the water was high.

So they said, "Come as quickly as you can and get out of here." So I said, "I'll get some dry clothes." I was putting in a bundle and I said to my brother, "You take Mary and the children and then come back for me. I'll be ready then." Mary said, "Ellen, you go. I'll finish that." She gave me the baby. He was two years old. She said, "Jim will come back for me." So I went.

Jim and I took Johnny. We went and the water was nearly to our knees. Before we got to the corner, the water was nearly up to our waist. The house was on the corner. At the end of our street there was a bayou. You could only go one way. That house was sitting in the middle of the street. We started from Forty-fourth and [Avenue] S½. In those days that was way down the Island. We went around this corner and there was a house across [Avenue] S. We called it Butcher Miller's house.[28] He owned that and the whole block of ground. It was an old colonial house with big columns. There were forty people in that house. It went to pieces. One lived. We didn't get there.

There were some people across the street who left their home at the same time we did. One of the women went to cross in that alley and the water took her like she was a chip of wood. So we didn't try to cross. We went into a house that was there. The people had abandoned it and had gone to this house that we were going to.

We were in this house with some of the neighbors. It was a two-story house and we were upstairs. There were two rooms down and two rooms up. Suddenly the window blew in and so they took the wardrobe and put it up against the window. That blew down like a little piece of paper. Then the gallery went. In a few minutes the house began to go.

I was sitting by a table and on that table was a watch. It was six o'clock and I had the baby. I had a quilt wrapped around him. He'd been sick with a fever all day. Suddenly the house went—just collapsed. We were underwater. I never moved. I was sitting on a chair, but when the house came up I was sitting on the floor. I had the baby, but he had slipped out of my arm and I just had him this way with his head. I said to one of the women, "Where's the baby? Help me quick. I'm losing him!" They helped put him back in my arms. We just sat there and drifted.

We drifted into a house that had an ell. This house had two big cisterns with good foundations. My brother said, "I don't want to be in another house that goes down. Let's get under these cisterns." I said, "Jim, I've got to get out of this rain. I've got to get Johnny out of this rain." That rain was like needles. It hurt so bad. Every once in a while the quilt would blow off of him, but he never said a word. He just put his little hands up to his face.

So we crawled into the window of this place. There were some mules

68. "We drifted into a house that had an ell. This house had two big cisterns with good foundations."—Ellen Edwards Nilson

in the bottom of this house. They had gone there for safety, but I don't know what happened to them. I wasn't interested in mules at the time. The people that owned the house had gone over to the Denver Resurvey school that was a brick building there.[29] They had abandoned their house. That night there were fifty souls killed in that school. It went to pieces.

As we went in, there was a woman and her two grown sons. We got in with her and these people were in the bed. They had taken off all their clothes. They were so wet and the bed was dry. I said to them, "Will you take the baby and warm him? He's got such a chill." They did and somebody took my clothes and wrung the water out of them and I put them back on. There wasn't any place on my body as big as your hand that wasn't bruised. I put my hand up and said, "My head's spinning." One of the men there said, "I thought the top of your head was gone the way it was bleeding."

We stayed there all night and poor little Johnny cried for water. The only water we had was what was leaking through the roof and the house was plastered. So you know how it tasted, but it was the only we had. I had always heard that at twelve o'clock it would be better or worse. So there was an alarm clock and man I watched it.

I could go to a window that looked out at the east. At twelve o'clock I couldn't see anything; it was just a sheet of water. I went back and I said, "Oh I see the ground." They said, "You're crazy." I said, "Come see." As soon as it got daylight, we got out of there and walked on dry ground.

Sunday morning we walked and we didn't know just where we were. So we walked down to the beach, down that way. Around us dead bodies were all over the ground. Somehow I knew that it wasn't any of mine. I wasn't worried. I just knew.

Aunt Perkins's house stood. It was on Thirty-seventh and [Avenue] I.[30] We went there and stayed for a while. There was one woman in there with us that had a six-week-old baby. She lost that baby three times in the water and grabbed it. That baby never whimpered the next day.

Auntie was a very efficient woman, but not a kind person. She said, "Where are the others?" and I said, "Auntie, I don't know." She said, "The Lord giveth and the Lord taketh away. Blessed be the name of the Lord." That was the wrong thing to say to me then, but that was her attitude to me all the time.

They all went. My oldest sister [Janey] and her husband had five children. Then the next sister [Mary] had two children. We had one. The next sister [Eliza] was not married. There was only fourteen months difference between us and we were always together. Then of course I had cousins. This cousin that had come up there, his wife was at our house then. They waited for Jim to take me and come back, but he never got back.

I went to look out the window the next morning and one of the women said, "Don't let her look out there." I said, "Why?" One of them spoke, "Give me the baby then." That was my cousin laying out there. That's the only body we ever found. My brother went and looked around but he couldn't find anybody.

If you were caught stooping, you might be shot. There was one man that when they took him he had his pockets full of ears and fingers. He didn't take time to take the earrings out of ears, he just cut a piece off. Of course by that time the fingers would be swollen. He just cut the fingers off and stuffed them in his pocket. He would have been shot, but his wife was pregnant and she begged for him. So they didn't shoot him.

The bodies were collected and put on barges and carried out to sea. They floated right back in. So they were burned. They made big piles of

69. Taking jewelry off of bodies to use later for identification. "If you were caught stooping, you might be shot."—Ellen Edwards Nilson

lumber and all over. I never got out because Johnny was so sick for three days and nights. I watched [him] and all he said was, "Mamma, mamma," until I kind of though[t] he wouldn't let anyone touch him but me.

KATHERINE VEDDER PAULS

Katherine Vedder, born in Galveston on December 19, 1894, was the youngest daughter of Charles A. Vedder and Florence Shryver. In 1899 the family moved to a home at Fifty-third and Avenue S in the new subdivision called Denver Resurvey. There were about thirty homes in that area at the time of the 1900 storm.

After the storm, Katherine and her older brother and sister were sent to her mother's family in Troy, New York, where she attended school. She later attended public school in Galveston as well as Kidd Key College in Sherman, Texas, where she studied music.

She married Cortes Pauls on January 8, 1916, and they made their home in Galveston. She played an active role in the preservation of Galveston history through her membership in the Galveston Historical Society in the 1950s. Susan Atherton interviewed Katherine Vedder Pauls on February 3, 1970 as part of a community research project under the direction of the Junior League.

On Friday afternoon, September 7, about five o'clock, we all stood on a little northeast gallery off the dining room. My father had heard that day in town of a hurricane in the Gulf and all scanned the sky for some sign of the approaching storm. It was a perfect late summer afternoon, the sky clear blue and cloudless. I saw a tiny cloud drifting from the southeast and asked eagerly, "Papa, is that the hurricane?"

On Saturday the eighth, Ella, our cook, prepared the Sunday dinner as usual. Everyone went about their usual tasks until about 11:00 a.m. when my brother, Jacob, eleven years of age, and our cousin, Allen Brooks, age thirteen, came from the beach with a report that the Gulf was very rough and the tide very high.

We all ate a sketchy lunch and waiting anxiously for my father to come home. Leaving town around noon, it took him nearly two hours to drive home, for by then the wind was rising rapidly and a steady rain had started. He was full of news of the approaching storm and immediately started preparing for what might come.

Two umbrella chinas flanking the front of the house were tied securely to the fence and then to the pillars of the front gallery. Blinds were tied together and everything with a lid was fastened down as tight as possible. Periodically the two boys ran the five blocks to the beach to see how much nearer the Gulf had come in.

Captain Minor, closest to the beach, felt secure in the concrete retaining wall he had constructed around his place.[31] His body was never found.

About half past three, Jacob and Allen came running, shouting excitedly that the Gulf looked like a great gray wall about fifty feet high and moving slowly toward the island. My father gathered us together and talked quietly to us. "This house is not as well built as the Richard Peek house, so all of us must put on our wool bathing suits to keep from being chilled. If the house goes down, make a human chain and follow me down the fence line to the Peek house."[32]

By 5 p.m. the tidal wave and the hurricane struck simultaneously and my father, seeing his family comparatively safe, set out in waist-deep water to look after his neighbors. In the frightening hours before darkness settled over the city, the water had come in over the tops of the four-foot fences.

People from homes already demolished were beginning to drift into our house, which still stood starkly against the increasing fury of the wind and water. The Masons soon came and with the family and a number of soldiers from Fort Crockett, all eventually totaling fifty, gathered in the front hall.[33] My father removed a closet door and the hall door leading to the kitchen and nailed them crosswise to reinforce the front door.

The women sat on the stairs and Kearny and Francesca Mason and I played in the hall near a cloak closet under the stairs. Suddenly there was a sensation such as one feels in a boat being lifted by a giant swell. The house rose, floated from its six-foot foundation and with a terrific jolt, settled on the ground. We children were submerged in five feet of water and the soldiers groping frantically about finally fished all three of us out and handed us, gasping and dripping, to our mothers, who had fled higher up the stairs.

I wept for my Papa, who took me on his back, where with arms and legs wrapped around his neck and waist, I stayed until the water reached nearly to his shoulders. Transferred to the comparative safety of the stairs, I called out, "Papa, there's my kitten." He pulled a soaking, clawing bit of fur from the water and tossed it up the stairs. Mrs. Mason caught it and shrieking, "It's a rat," tossed it back into the water. It was sometime before the kitten was safe in my arms.

The water rose higher and the women moved up the stairs. The roof had blown off of the two east bedrooms and rain was pouring in. A bathroom on the west side of the house was dry, and it was here that twelve or fifteen people spent the night in some degree of comfort. Francesca and I were very sleepy and my mother found a bedspread and laid it in the tub and there we two little girls curled up and slept part of the night. Downstairs, the situation was dangerous.

Construction of a new barracks at Fort Crockett had necessitated the use of twelve-by-twelve-inch beams some twenty feet long and these floating through the water were like battering rams against the newly built homes. When my father realized this, he again nailed the doors, loosened by the settling of the house, to the space where the front door had been.

Standing with his powerful arms reaching through the aperture, [he] pushed the beams away as they floated close to the house, thus averting the terrible damage they would have caused. Undoubtedly this action saved our home and its occupants, but for months after he suffered agony as the doctor probed and worked over his torn and lacerated arms and hands, for they were filled with glass, splinters, and other foreign matter which swept by on the waters of the storm. His fingers bore the scars to the rest of his life.

Sometime during the early morning hours a cry for help came and from the dark and muddy water were brought Mr. and Mrs. Collum, [and] Captain Thomas Longineau, his wife, and [their] six-week-old baby, Tom. The Longineau's baby was unconscious and Mrs. Longineau cried out that her baby was dead. My mother took him and saw that there was still a spark of life. She crawled on her hands and knees through the darkness into the northeast room where, from an overturned bureau and cabinet, she pulled a knitted woolen petticoat and a broken bottle of blackberry cordial.

Making her way back in the pitch black dark, she stripped the baby of its wet clothing and wrapped it in the woolen garment and placed the now dry and purring kitten next to the baby's body for warmth. Pouring the cordial into a toothbrush mug, she told Mrs. Longineau to take some of it in her mouth with her teeth together, to keep out any broken glass, and then to put it drop by drop into the baby's mouth. This she did and gradually the tiny cold body grew warm and soon a wailing infant demanded food.

About daylight the storm began to subside, the waters to recede. As the light came, a call from outside brought help from the house and in shocked silence they saw standing stripped stark naked, except for a piece of mattress ticking, their neighbor Captain Munn.[34] His home, his wife, and her mother were all gone. He had floated all night on a mattress and so was saved. As friendly sympathetic hands drew him into shelter, tears streamed down his face and there are no words to describe his desolation.

Mr. Mason waded out the north side of the house and in the half light saw his home, but there was no home to be found. All that was left was part of a brick storeroom on whose shelf sat in defiance of wind and wave, a lone bottle of beer and a can of sardines.

There was no smile on any face when daylight brought a clear view of the yard. My mother's first glance out of the window showed a little dead Negro child, its body entangled in the debris in the yard. Though she and all of us became familiar with the sight of violent death in the next few hours, to her that still, small, brown form epitomized the storm.

There was little talk. All were stunned by the catastrophe that had overtaken them. They gazed in silence at the desolate devastation. Then Jacob cried out, "Papa, where are the Peeks?" Everyone looked to the west where their neighbors' home had stood. Not a plank nor brick remained. Not even a trace of the foundation. Richard Peek, his wife, eight children, and two servants were gone. To this day their bodies have never been found. My father said in shocked tones, "And it was to their house that I would have taken you all for refuge."

Some higher power had kept the Vedder family in their home, one of only three houses left standing in that once thriving suburb. The rain and wind abated, the waters receded and by afternoon our family and a number of others decided to attempt to make their way into town. The horrors of the trip are almost indescribable.

Clad in bathing suits we made our difficult way toward the beach where the debris was less high. No streets or roads were visible. The wreckage piled high obscured every familiar landmark. We picked our way where we could, sometimes in ankle-deep water and mud, sometimes in water waist deep where great holes had been created by the current.

I walked where the water was shallow, but most of the long journey I had to be carried. As we walked we exchanged snatches of conversation. One would say, "I wonder how this or that family came through." Along the road they saw a bicycle stuck up in the mud and sitting jauntily on it, hat on head and cigar in mouth, was a dead Negro man.

Closer into town they saw an overturned cabinet and on the top shelf, wrapped in a quilt, the lifeless form of a boy of about three years. And most poignant of all, a nun with several children tied to her body.[35] Their minds became numb to the horrors and they stumbled on in silence.

My mother carried in her hand her jewelry in a small chamois bag. Once she stepped on a barrel concealed by the water. It rolled and she went under with it, losing her grasp on the bag. She groped frantically about and finally found it. She grabbed at something to pull herself up. It was the body of a small girl. Her self-control gave way and she wept hysterically.

The group turned in from the beach at Thirty-fifth Street and made

70. "Every day my parents drove out to Denver to salvage what they could."
—Katherine Vedder Pauls

their way to Avenue O, then over to Thirty-third and on to Broadway. Broadway was comparatively clear and at the end of a five-hour walk we were at my grandparents door on Twenty-eighth Street and Broadway.[36] I sat on the steps and cried, for I didn't want my grandmother to see me in my little wet red bathing suit. Once inside, Grandmother Vedder gave us hot coffee and bowls of hot grits with butter melting in little pools in the middle. Nothing before or since ever tasted so good.

For many days it was impossible to get back to their wrecked home, but on September nineteenth, eleven days after the storm, my parents made a trip to see what could be salvaged. As they went into the backyard, they saw the icebox standing upright by the kitchen steps. Opening the door, my mother exclaimed as she drew out the Sunday roast intact but covered with a thick coat of mud.

Every day my parents drove out to Denver [Resurvey] to salvage what they could of the home furnishings. While digging around in the yard, my mother managed to unearth more than three dozen pieces of Haveline china, which buried in the soft mud came out without a scratch or chip. This was her wedding china.

My father made plans to send us north while the city was cleared of debris and free from threat of epidemic.

Many years later I was on a bus going from New York to Philadelphia. A young lady came down and sat by me and asked me if I minded her smoking. When I answered her, she said, "You're from the South aren't you?"

I said, "Yes, I'm from Galveston, Texas."

"Oh," she said, "my grandparents used to run the Beach Hotel in Galveston, but after it burned they came north and I have been living with them in New York." She said, "You know, my grandmother told me the most fantastic story."

I said, "What was it?"

She said, "She told me about a home down the island where a lot of people spent the night of the storm and there was a little baby that was brought in just about dead and the lady who lived in the home saved the little baby. She wrapped him in a woolen petticoat and gave him some cordial and brought the little baby back to life." And she said, "Isn't that the most remarkable thing?"

I said, "Well, you don't know how remarkable it is, because it was in my home that the baby was saved and it was my mother who saved him."

NOTES

PREFACE

1. Green, Nathan C., *Story of the Galveston Flood,* p. 3.

INTRODUCTION

1. William A. Scharnweber, ed., *Facts about Galveston, Texas, the Deep Water Harbor of the Gulf of Mexico,* p. 65.
2. *Galveston Daily News,* January 1, 1899, p. 10. Galveston's emergence as a deep-water port during the latter half of the nineteenth century is told by Earle B. Young in *Galveston and the Great West.*
3. Clarence Ousley, ed., *Galveston in Nineteen Hundred: The Authorized and Official Record of the Proud City of the Southwest as It Was before and after the Hurricane of September 8, and a Logical Forecast of Its Future,* pp. 150–51, 156.
4. *Morrison and Fourmy's General Directory of the City of Galveston, 1899–1900,* p. 4.
5. Brownson Malsch, *Indianola: The Mother of Western Texas,* pp. 235–37. This was the first severe hurricane to strike the Texas coast since the state had been settled en masse. Malsch notes that its wind gusts reached an estimated 150 miles per hour. Hurricanes are graded in intensity according to their sustained winds. An *extreme* hurricane has sustained winds greater than 135 miles per hour. The 1900 storm that struck Galveston was, by contrast, a *major* storm (winds between 100 and 135 miles per hour) since its maximum wind velocity was estimated to be around 120 miles per hour. See Walter K. Henry, Dennis M. Driscoll, and J. Patrick McCormack, *Hurricanes on the Texas Coast,* pp. 16–23, for an explanation of the destructive effects of hurricanes, including winds, storm surge, and flooding.
6. Malsch, *Indianola,* pp. 262–66.
7. Clarence Ousley placed the most conservative estimate of deaths at six thousand victims in Galveston, a thousand more on Galveston Island, and yet another thousand on the mainland; see Ousley, *Nineteen Hundred,* p. 265. David G. McComb, in *Galveston: A History,* p. 122, concurs with Ousley's estimate of six thousand dead in Galveston. The Rosenberg Library's 1900 storm Web page (http://rosenberg-library.org/gthc/1900storm.htm) features an index to over five thousand victims.

8. E. R. Cheesborough, "Commission Plan Success in Galveston," 1908; George Kibbe Turner, "Galveston: A Business Corporation;" 1906; and "Galveston's Commission Form of Government," n.d., all in the Subject File, Rosenberg Library, Galveston and Texas History Center, Galveston, Tex.
9. Henry M. Robert (1837–1923), who served in the U.S. Army, had experience in building fortifications and improving waterways. In 1876, he authored *A Pocket Manual of Rules of Order for Deliberative Assemblies,* popularly known as "Robert's Rules of Order." Alfred Noble (1844–1914) was a consulting engineer from Chicago. In 1895, Pres. Grover Cleveland appointed him to the Nicaragua Canal Commission. From 1897 to 1900 Noble also served as a member of the Deep Water Commission, which examined the feasibility of a canal between the Great Lakes and the Atlantic Ocean, and with the Isthmian Canal Commission from 1899 to 1903. Henry C. Ripley was a consulting engineer who specialized in harbor improvements.
10. In Galveston, the storm surge from the 1900 hurricane reached a maximum height of almost sixteen feet. This figure is nearly double the height of the storm surge for the 1875 Galveston hurricane. See Frank Thomas Harrowing, "The Galveston storm of 1900" (Master's thesis, University of Houston, 1950), p. 56. The storm surge is a dome of water that is driven along by a hurricane's winds. It claimed the lives of many of Galveston's residents who lived along the beach and did not evacuate in time.
11. Albert M. Davis, Jr., "Galveston's Bulwark against the Sea: History of the Galveston Seawall," paper presented at the 2d Annual Conference on Coastal Engineering, Houston, Tex., Nov., 1951, pp. 2–4.
12. S. C. Griffin, *History of Galveston, Texas: Narrative and Biographical,* pp. 76–77, 80, 84.
13. McComb, *Galveston,* pp. 150–51; and Harrowing, "Galveston Storm," p. 167.
14. Murat Halstead, *Galveston: The Horrors of a Stricken City; Portraying by Pen and Picture the Awful Calamity that Befell the Queen City on the Gulf and the Terrible Scenes that Followed the Disaster,* pp. 99, 157, 177.
15. Ibid., p. 91.
16. Paul Lester, *The Great Galveston Disaster: Containing a Full and Thrilling Account of the Most Appalling Calamity of Modern Times,* pp. 65, 238.
17. Ousley, *Galveston in Nineteen Hundred,* p. 275.
18. Erik Larson, *Isaac's Storm: A Man, a Time, and the Deadliest Hurricane in History,* pp. 15, 197.
19. Ibid., p. 198.
20. Beverley Raphael, *When Disaster Strikes: How Individuals and Communities Cope with Catastrophe,* pp. 61–63.
21. Ibid., pp. 72–73, 93.
22. Ibid., pp. 72–73.
23. Peter E. Hodgkinson and Michael Stewart, *Coping with Catastrophe: A Handbook of Post-Disaster Psychosocial Aftercare,* p. 7.

24. Saundra K. Schneider, *Flirting with Disaster: Public Management in Crisis Situations*, p. 51.
25. Tim Newburn, *Disaster and After: Social Work in the Aftermath of Disaster*, pp. 58, 60.
26. Raphael, *When Disaster Strikes*, pp. 74–75.
27. Ibid., pp. 80–82.
28. Schneider, *Flirting with Disaster*, pp. 51–52.
29. Raphael, *When Disaster Strikes*, pp. 94–95.

SURVIVOR LETTERS

1. John Blagden lost track of the days. The storm occurred on Saturday night.
2. The U.S. Weather Service was located at the E. S. Levy Building at 2227 Avenue D (Market), on the corner of Twenty-third and Avenue D (Market).
3. Dr. Cline and his family lived at 2511 Avenue Q.
4. Borncasiel was also listed as T. C. Bornkessell in the U.S. Weather Bureau report. He was not recorded in the city directory for 1899–1900, but he and his wife were listed among the dead.
5. Maggie Robinson, a fifty-four-year-old widow, was born in England. She lived at 2214 Avenue H with Kate Jenkins, a forty-one-year-old single woman.
6. The Adoue and Lobit Bank was located at 2102 Avenue B (Strand).
7. George's brother, John D. Hodson, also worked for the insurance company. Alphonse Kennison, according to the 1899–1900 city directory, lived at 1120 Twenty-third (Tremont) Street.
8. J. Edwin Vieno worked as a stenographer with George Hodson. He lived at 2616 Avenue H (Ball).
9. Herman Marwitz built his home at 2203 Avenue H (Ball) in 1893, but he never lived in it. Despite his financial success as president of the Street Railway Company and the Galveston Savings Bank, he almost went bankrupt with the construction costs. The "Marwitz Castle," as it came to be known, was leased and Marwitz died in 1899. During the 1900 storm it was in use as a ladies rooming house. The First Baptist Church purchased the residence to use for their Sunday school, but it was demolished in 1969.
10. Mae, Charles, and John Conlon lived at 1604 Thirty-first Street.
11. Fannie Peacock lived at 1620 Avenue E (Postoffice).
12. This part of the letter begins on page two of a letter started to her sister.
13. Richard Wilson, a forty-one-year-old widower, worked as a servant for the Davis family.
14. Attorney Marcus Mott lived at 1119 Twenty-third (Tremont) Street, east of the Davis family home.
15. Walter Gresham's residence, located on the corner of Fourteenth Street and Broadway, is now known as the "Bishop's Palace." The Sealy residence, also known by the name "Open Gates" and located at Twenty-fifth Street and Broadway, is now owned by the University of Texas Medical Branch.

16. Denver Resurvey encompassed about 660 acres between Broadway and the Gulf, and Forty-fifth and Fifty-seventh Streets. After being resurveyed in 1890, a number of Colorado investors joined two Galvestonians in the Galveston Land and Improvement Company to develop this area into a residential neighborhood.
17. All of these families lived in the Denver Resurvey area. Many of these families are mentioned in more than one letter, as they were well known around the island.
18. For an account of the experiences of Mrs. W. H. Heideman, see Herbert Malloy Mason. *Death from the Sea: Our Greatest Natural Disaster, the Galveston Hurricane of 1900*, p. 155–58.
19. Ritter's Saloon was located at 2109 Avenue B (Strand). Stanley Spencer, a well-known Philadelphia realtor, was visiting his Galveston office to meet with Richard "Dick" Lord, another realtor.
20. Isabella Kopperl was a neighbor living at Twenty-fourth and Broadway.
21. Waters S. and Daisy Davis were Sarah's brother- and sister-in-law.
22. Dr. Arthur Sampson was the family doctor who attended the birth of Harry, Jr., in April, 1900.
23. Richard Spillane was the city editor of the *Galveston Tribune.*
24. A chiffonier is an ornamental dresser or chest of drawers.
25. The Sweeney house was located across the street at 2402 Avenue L. Mrs. Sweeney was living at her parent's home, Ashton Villa, at the time of the storm.
26. This account is incorrect. The man and his family floated during the storm on Saturday night.
27. Quicklime is a white powdery substance placed over the dead to prevent the spread of disease.
28. The Aziola Club was a social and literary society incorporated in April, 1890. At the time of the storm it had eighty-five members and its offices were on the second floor of 2225 Avenue E (Postoffice).
29. Brogans are a heavy, coarse, leather shoe reaching to the ankle.
30. The Citizens' Committee was organized by Mayor Walter Jones to relieve suffering after the storm. He assigned a chairman to each Galveston ward to be responsible for providing food, organizing workers, and clearing debris. This approach later led to Galveston adopting the city commission form of government in 1901.
31. Walter C. Jones (1848–1906) came to Galveston as a young boy. He clerked for White and Ledyard as a young man and became successful doing contract work for the Gulf, Colorado, and Santa Fe Railroad. He spent nine years at his birthplace in Colorado County, Texas, farming before returning to Galveston in 1889. He became the chief of police in 1895 and served in that post until he was elected mayor in June, 1899. His role in organizing Galveston's city government after the 1900 storm was extremely important. Jones died suddenly of a pulmonary embolism in 1906.
32. Edwin N. Ketchum (1843–1931) came to Texas after serving with the Union army

during the Civil War. He served as a clerk in the Texas legislature before settling in Galveston in 1872 in the contracting business. He served as the chief of police after Walter C. Jones became mayor in 1899. After the storm, he worked for the Galveston customhouse.

33. George Hardie, a cotton broker, lived at 1724 Avenue K.
34. William Schirmer, a mailman, lived at 1827 Avenue N½.
35. The Knights of Pythias, a fraternal order, had nine lodges organized in Galveston. The Masons had five lodges in Galveston.
36. Chapman also means a customer.
37. Virginia Point is the point of the mainland that connects the railroad bridge and current causeway to Galveston Island.
38. Galveston schools resumed classes on October 22, 1900.
39. Walter Gresham, a Galveston attorney and congressional representative, began construction on his residence at Fourteenth and Broadway in 1886. Designed by Nicholas Clayton, it cost more than $250,000. After Gresham died in 1920, Mrs. Gresham sold the residence to the Galveston-Houston Catholic Diocese for Bishop Christopher Byrne, who lived there until his own death in 1950. During this time the residence became known as the Bishop's Palace. Today it is the only Texas building recognized by the American Institute of Architecture as being one of the one hundred outstanding buildings in the United States.
40. Archibald Campbell, a Galveston attorney, lived at 1515 Broadway.
41. Bertha Lobit lived at 1527 Broadway, on the corner of Sixteenth and Broadway, with her husband, Joseph, and six children.
42. Miss Hertford was referring to the main esplanade on Broadway.
43. Mrs. Brown's residence was Ashton Villa, 2326 Broadway.
44. J. H. Hawley worked at 301 Twenty-third (Tremont) Street and lived at 1416 Avenue H (Ball).
45. Woollam's Lake, a popular beer garden, was located at the corner of Forty-first and Avenue Q, next to the John W. Harris homestead.
46. Harriet V. Wakelee was the widow of David Wakelee.
47. Walter Fisher worked as a prescription clerk for Broadway druggist J. J. Schott. He and Lillie Harris lived in the Denver Resurvey at 2204 Forty-first Street. Richard Swain was a cashier for cotton factor and merchant John D. Rogers.
48. The Davenport family lived in the Denver Resurvey at 3924 Avenue R. Cora Davenport, Lillie Fisher, and Rebecca Harris were the daughters of Annie and John Woods Harris. Their nephew, John W. Harris, has an account in the oral history section.
49. William A. McVitie, vice-president of the Galveston Maritime Association, served on the Citizens' Committee, which was responsible for cleaning the city and giving supplies to the survivors.
50. Robert Bradley Hawley, the U.S. congressional representative from Galveston, was Joseph H. Hawley's brother.
51. William R. Johnson was a real estate agent, U.S. commissioner, notary public, and commissioner of deeds.

52. This is Ashton Villa.
53. The Willis residence, later known as Moody Mansion, was built by Narcissus Willis, the mother-in-law of J. H. Hawley's daughter.
54. E. D. Cavin served as a judge in the Galveston and Harris County Criminal District Court. He and his family lived at 3314 Avenue O.
55. Dr. William Fisher, the city health officer, lived at 1725 Avenue I (Sealy).
56. Stanley Spencer, the real estate broker from Philadelphia, was one of the four men Sarah Hawley mentioned being killed at Ritter's Saloon downtown.
57. Edwin E. Rice, a fire insurance agent, lived at 2627 Broadway.
58. Waters S. Davis, Jr., was Sarah Hawley's brother.
59. Mrs. Anna Masterson, whose husband, Branch T., was a Galveston attorney, lived at 3902 Avenue R.
60. For a biography of Miss Bettie Brown of Ashton Villa, see Sherrie McLeRoy, *Daughter of Fortune: The Bettie Brown Story.*
61. Oak Lawn was a popular name for the Austin residence at 1502 Avenue D (Market).
62. Brush Electric Light and Power Company had a powerhouse on the southwest corner of Twenty-sixth and Avenue E (Postoffice). The Galveston Gas Company works was located on the southwest corner of Thirty-second and Avenue D (Market). The city's water supply came from thirty artesian wells located at Alta Loma on the mainland. Galveston's first water plant was established in 1892 and the city's pump house and reservoir were located between Thirtieth and Thirty-first Streets and Avenue G (Winnie) and Avenue H (Ball).
63. Richard H. Peek, who is mentioned in other accounts, was from Mrs. Austin's hometown of Lexington, Virginia. He and his family lived near the Vedder family at 5408 Avenue S in the Denver Resurvey. Katherine Vedder Pauls mentions them in her account of the storm.

SURVIVOR MEMOIRS

1. Major Fayling had not been in Galveston long before the storm. There is no street named Midway, although Twenty-first Street was known as Center Street, and Twenty-third Street as Tremont. Twenty-fifth Street had very recently been renamed Rosenberg Street in honor of Henry Rosenberg, who died in 1893. It is possible that Major Fayling was on one of these three streets. O'Keefe's bathing pavilion was at the end of Twenty-third Street, the Pagoda was at the end of Twenty-fourth Street and Murdoch's was at Twenty-fifth Street.
2. The Young Men's Christian Association (YMCA) Building was located on the southwest corner of Twenty-third (Tremont) and Avenue G (Winnie).
3. Dr. William H. Baldinger was an ear, nose, and throat specialist. Dr. William Nave, only twenty-two years old, lived with his two sisters at 2403 Avenue M. The Gill and League Building was located on the southeast corner of Twenty-first and Avenue D (Market).
4. The Four Seasons restaurant stood at 318 Twenty-first Street.

5. Rev. James M. Kirwin (1872–1926), born in Circleville, Ohio, began serving the people of Galveston as rector of Saint Mary's Cathedral in 1896. In 1898 he was elected chaplain of the First U.S. Volunteer Infantry Regiment, which he had helped organize. His efforts after the 1900 storm brought him attention and prominence among the citizens of Galveston.
6. Capt. W. C. Rafferty commanded Battery O, First Artillery at Fort Crockett. Located in the Denver Resurvey, Fort Crockett had a heavy battery of ten-inch guns and mortars. Captain Rafferty lost twenty-eight men. See John Edward Weems, *A Weekend in September,* p. 62.
7. Thomas Scurry (1859–1911), appointed adjutant general by Gov. Charles Culberson in 1899, arrived in Galveston to supervise martial law. He was captain of the Houston Light Guards from 1880 to 1886, and served as a major in the First Texas Volunteer Infantry during the Spanish-American War.
8. Notice in Sarah Davis Hawley's letter of September 12 that she had armed herself with a pistol to protect their property from looters.
9. John Sealy, Jr., (1870–1926), a full partner in the Hutchings-Sealy Bank, helped lead the management of relief operations in Galveston after the storm. He is best remembered as founder of the John Sealy Hospital, which he named for his father.
10. The Hutchins House, located at 907 Franklin Avenue in Houston, was owned by William T. Boyle and John T. Boyle. They both worked as real estate agents, ran two hotels in Houston, and shared a home in the Heights neighborhood.
11. Drummers are traveling salesmen.
12. The Johnston, Pennsylvania, flood occurred on May 31, 1889, after heavy rains broke through a dam. The death toll numbered over two thousand.
13. Gen. W. H. Sears accompanied Clara Barton to Galveston and assisted her in assessing the damage on the mainland and distributing supplies to survivors.
14. Louis J. Tuffly, mayor pro-tem of Houston, was coproprietor of Krupp-Tuffly, a boot and shoe business.
15. First Lady Ida Saxton McKinley suffered from epilepsy and Pres. William McKinley had a reputation for his great devotion and tender affection towards her.
16. Martial law ended at noon on September 21 according to a proclamation by Mayor Jones, who acted on Brig. Gen. Thomas Scurry's recommendation.
17. The Dallas Rough Riders, led by Capt. Ormond Paget, were Troop B, First Squadron, First Cavalry, stationed in Dallas in 1900. Forty-five members arrived in Galveston on Saturday, September 12.
18. Clarence Ousley (1863–1948) worked for the *Galveston Tribune* at the time of the storm. In 1903 he established the *Fort Worth Record.* He dedicated proceeds from his account of the storm, *Galveston in Nineteen Hundred,* to the reconstruction of the city's public schools.
19. Ben Stuart refers to similar tropical storms that struck Galveston on September 16, 1875, and October 19, 1886.
20. The Beach Hotel, designed by Nicholas Clayton in 1883, stood at the end of Twenty-third (Tremont) Street and the Beach. Although a very popular resort,

it consistently lost money and eventually had to be sold for taxes. On the morning of July 23, 1898, the hotel, constructed entirely of wood, burned to the ground.

21. Charles H. McMaster served on the Board of Water Commissioners after the storm. He was also secretary of the Galveston Chamber of Commerce, and treasurer for the *Galveston Tribune.*
22. William G. Sterett worked for the *Dallas (Morning) News* as an editor. At the time of the 1900 storm, the *Galveston News* was the parent company of the *Dallas News.*
23. Gen. Chambers McKibben, commander of the Department of Texas, arrived during the evening of September 11, 1900. He came under the order of the Secretary of War.
24. The *Galveston News* Building, located at 2108 Avenue C (Mechanic), continued to house the newspaper until 1965, when it moved to its current location at Teichman's Point.
25. Thirty-five-year-old Beulah Gaither was the assistant matron at the Galveston Orphan's Home on the west side of Twenty-first Street between Avenues M and M½. Ethel Gaither, nineteen, worked as an assistant and teacher.
26. Mrs. Rollfing had the date confused. The night before the storm was Friday, September 7.
27. The Rollfings lived at 1723 Eighteenth Street, on the corner of Avenue O½.
28. Frank Malloy's livery and boarding stables were located at 2321 Avenue E (Postoffice).
29. George Reyder, a grocer, lived at 3602 Broadway.
30. A woman and her family walking from Thirty-sixth and Broadway to Forty-first and Avenue F (Church) would surely have seen human bodies. Her assertion is difficult to believe in light of the staggering loss of life the previous day and evening.
31. Frederick Viehman, a cistern builder, lived at 4111 Avenue F (Church).
32. William and Fred Rollfing were August Rollfing's brothers.
33. Portieres are curtains that hang over doorways.
34. Vincenz Juenger, a contract painter and paperhanger, and his family lived in Houston at 1101 La Branch.
35. Wolfram traveled down Twenty-third (Tremont) Street to Broadway, crossed Broadway and then traveled six blocks west to Twenty-ninth Street.
36. The iron picket fence surrounded the Galveston Artillery Club at the southwest corner of Twenty-third (Tremont) and Broadway.
37. The Texas Heroes Monument, dedicated to those who fought at the Battle of San Jacinto, stands at the intersection of Broadway and Twenty-fifth Street. Henry Rosenberg, a Swiss immigrant who left his fortune to fund various charitable institutions throughout Galveston, provided for the monument in his will. The dedication ceremony took place on April 21, 1900.
38. Edwin E. Rice was a fire insurance agent and part owner of Rice, Baulard, and Company, which dealt in paints and wallpaper. His residence was at 2627 Broadway at the southeast corner of Twenty-seventh and Broadway.

39. The Cortes residence was at 3123 Avenue N.
40. Cortes failed to remember that his grandfather, Henry Cortes, died April 10, 1899, a year and a half before the storm.
41. The Star Drug Store was originally located on the southeast corner of Twenty-third Street and Avenue E (Postoffice). It moved next door to 510 Twenty-third (Tremont) Street between 1916 and 1919. On March 12, 1998, the Star Drug Store closed after a heavy fire damaged its building and destroyed the corner building.
42. Frank and Alma Walker lived at 3127 Avenue P½, only five blocks south of the Cortes residence.
43. Hardtack is a hard biscuit or loaf bread made of flour and water without salt.
44. The U.S. Weather Bureau journal for September 7 makes no mention of rain, only rough seas. Ida Smith Austin, in an earlier letter, mentions the beautiful moonlit night on Friday evening.
45. Maxson's claim that a British counselor built the home cannot be confirmed. The Maxson family rented and moved twice between 1899 and 1900. The description of the home resembles 3918 Avenue M½, which was built in 1896 for C. Leopold Biehler, the owner of a meat market. In 1900 Biehler lived in Eureka Springs, Arkansas, and may have rented the home to the Maxsons.
46. J. Forrest Runge (1892–1964) was the son of Louis and Anna Focke Runge, who lived at 1228 Market. According to additional information in the William Maury Darst Papers, MSS# 93-0023, Box 2-3, Forrest sat on a marble topped dresser situated in the middle of a large piece of flooring which floated him from the East End to the Maxson house at Fortieth and Avenue M½.
47. The correct name for the store was Focke, Wilkens, and Lange, 2110 Avenue B (Strand).
48. Col. Hunt McCaleb was an aide to Brig. Gen. Thomas Scurry.
49. All railroad trestles connected Galveston Island with the Texas mainland at Virginia Point.
50. Walter Scott Mayer, sixteen, lived at 1404 Thirty-ninth Street with his mother, Uncle Henry Mayer, and grandmother. His sister is not listed with the family in the 1900 census.
51. Robert and Geneva Scholes had a year-old son, Robert D. Scholes, and lived at 2709 Avenue H (Ball). Geneva's mother, Marsaline, a widow, lived with her six-year-old daughter, Frances, at 2618 Avenue L.
52. "Little Town Park," properly known as League Park, is located in League City on the mainland. John C. League (1849–1916) set aside the land for the park when he was laying out the town site. The park, established in 1895, included a two-story bandstand.
53. Charles G. Dibrell, Geneva's sixteen-year-old brother, later studied law at night, passed the Bar Exam in 1914, and was appointed judge of the Fifty-sixth District Court in 1926. He served twenty-seven years as the District Judge and County Juvenile Court Judge until his retirement in 1954. From then until his death in 1961 he served as chairman of the Galveston County Navigation District.

54. Alexander Wright lived on the mainland with his wife, Ella, and their two children, James, age two, and four-month-old Oliver.
55. Geneva Scholes was mistaken. Clyde Corrigan, who later went by the name Douglas, was not born until 1907. He earned the nickname "Wrong Way" Corrigan when he flew from New York to Ireland in 1938 after filing a flight plan for California. Corrigan's parents are not listed in the 1900 Galveston County federal census or Galveston city directory.
56. The 1915 storm struck Galveston on August 16–17. Approximately 275 people lost their lives and damage in Galveston amounted to $50 million. While this storm is considered to be more severe than the 1900 storm, the seawall and grade raising of Galveston are credited with saving additional lives and property.
57. James Grandison, forty-nine, lived with his wife, Julia, at 2606 Avenue E (Postoffice). According to the 1900 census they had three children, but they are not listed with their parents.
58. An ell is the extension to the main house, which is at a right angle, forming the shape of the letter L.
59. Frank and Anna Wagstaff lived at 2709 Avenue H (Ball).

SURVIVOR ORAL HISTORIES

1. Twenty-seven-year-old William Chappell Beal worked for the Galveston Waterworks.
2. The Williams-Tucker residence was located at 3601 Avenue P. Samuel May Williams, merchant, had his house partially prefabricated in Maine and brought to Galveston in 1839 aboard a schooner. The Williams family retained the house until 1859, when Philip Crosby Tucker became the owner. The Tucker family kept the house until 1954, when the Galveston Historical Foundation purchased the property and opened the restored house as a museum.
3. Fenelon Cannon, president of the F. Cannon Commission Company, resided at 3815 Avenue P. The company was located at 2309 Avenue B (Strand).
4. The Hendley Building, constructed in 1859 by William Hendley and Company, consisted of four identical buildings sharing common interior walls located on Avenue B (Strand) between Twentieth and Twenty-first Streets. The Galveston Historical Foundation's Strand Visitors' Center and other businesses currently occupy the first floor.
5. Ritter's Saloon and Restaurant was across the street and one block west at 2109 Avenue B (Strand).
6. Galveston's city hall, designed by architect Alfred Muller, was constructed in 1888. It stood three stories high, with a farmers' market on the first floor and local government offices on the second and third floors. After the 1900 storm, only the first and second floors were rebuilt and the police and fire departments were housed on the first floor until the building was torn down in 1966.
7. Charles H. Bader's meat market was located at 2023 Avenue N.
8. Julius Rowan was seventeen months old during the storm.

9. Dorothy "Dora" Wallstein, widow of Samuel Wallstein, lived at 1213 Thirteenth Street with three of her sons, George, Phillip, and Samuel. All three men were employed as house movers.
10. Grandmother Wallstein most likely ended up at Saint Mary's University located just behind Sacred Heart Catholic Church. The church was completely destroyed.
11. Sylvan Miller, a clerk, was one of six boarders in the Block house.
12. The 1899–1900 Galveston city directory lists Leopold Block as an employee of Bonart and Schornstein Clothiers at 2405 Market (Avenue D).
13. Twenty-year-old Henry Block worked for Miller Brothers, a manufacturer of and wholesale dealer in clothing. The company was located at 2219 Avenue C (Mechanic).
14. Richard W. Wolston (1852–1922) established R. W. Wolston and Company, which sold wholesale grains, and also owned Wolston's Stable, located at 2310 Avenue E (Postoffice). He was elected county commissioner for Precinct 3 six times, and served on the finance, public buildings, and road and bridges committee. He later served as the city commissioner for finance and revenue. His son, Clinton M. Wolston, worked for R.W. Wolston and Company and lived at 1426 Avenue F (Church).
15. Dan Kane worked as a boilermaker for Kane and Clark Boilermakers and lived at 3209 Avenue G (Winnie).
16. Right Rev. Nicholas A. Gallagher (1846–1917) became bishop of the Galveston Diocese in 1882.
17. This story cannot be confirmed, but Clara Barton arrived in Galveston on September 17. Rose Block was then eight years old.
18. The Mensing Building on the corner of Twenty-second and Avenue B (Strand) was owned by the Mensing brothers, who dealt in wholesale imports and cotton.
19. For an account of the Bristol family at home, see Mary Louise Bristol Hopkins's oral history.
20. This may have been Alexander Russell, a telegraph operator for the Santa Fe Railroad. His family lived at 1620 Twenty-fifth Street, between Avenue N½ and Avenue O.
21. Shotgun houses were cottages one room wide and arranged in a line, one room behind the other. They were called shotgun houses because if a person stood on the front porch and fired a shotgun, the shot would pass through all of the rooms.
22. Annie P. Harris, John's grandmother, lived at 2204 Forty-first Street, on the corner of Forty-first and Avenue Q½, with her two daughters, Miss Rebecca Harris and Mrs. Lillie Harris Fisher. Another daughter, Mrs. Cora Davenport, lived at 3924 Avenue R. Walter and Lillie Harris Fisher and Wharton and Cora Davenport had four children each in their families.
23. Louise (7) lived with her mother, sister, Lois (15), and older brothers John W. S. (24) and William M. (21). William Mason Bristol's account appears earlier.
24. A baluster is a short support like a column as in a stair rail.

25. Frederick Dau, of Germany, and his wife, Marie, had five children ranging in age from two to ten years.
26. James "Jim" Edwards was employed by the Galveston Police Department.
27. Mary and Frank Quinn lived at 728 Avenue M with sons William, age three, and John, age twenty-two months. Frank's widowed mother, Ellen, also lived with the family.
28. William P. Miller, manager of the Galveston Meat Company, lived at 2417 Forty-third Street on the corner of Avenue S. He and his wife were among the thousands of storm victims.
29. The Denver Resurvey School stood at Fiftieth and Avenue R.
30. Liza Perkins, a sister to Charity Edwards, lived at 3711 Avenue I (Sealy) with her husband, William, and two boarders.
31. Lucian Minor and his wife, Annie, lived at Fifty-fourth Street and Avenue X (on the beach) with their four children.
32. Richard H. Peek, who is mentioned in many earlier accounts, lived with his wife, Alice, and their children at 5408 Avenue S.
33. Kearny and Virginia Mason lived at Fifty-third Street and Avenue R with their three children, a servant and Mrs. Mason's sister. Kearny and Francesca Mason, who played with Katherine during the storm, were seven and four years old.
34. Capt. James W. Munn lived on Avenue S½ between Fifty-fourth and Fifty-fifth Streets with his parents and wife. All but he were lost.
35. Saint Mary's Orphanage, located on the beach four miles from Twenty-third (Tremont) Street, or approximately Sixty-third Street, consisted of two large two-story dormitories. At the time of the storm, there were ninety-three orphans and ten Sisters of Charity living there. In an attempt to save the children, each sister tied six to eight children to herself with a clothesline. All were killed, with the exception of three older boys: Will Murney, Frank Madera, and Albert Campbell.
36. Jacob and Margaret Vedder resided at 2725 Broadway with their daughter and son-in-law, Julia and Brewer Key.

BIBLIOGRAPHY

ARCHIVAL SOURCES

Galveston Independent School District Board of Trustees Minute Book. Vol. 5.

Houston Public Library, Houston Metropolitan Research Center, Houston, Texas. Houston City Council Minutes, Book K, June 19, 1899–February 4, 1901, p. 348. Microfilm Box no. 5.

Texas Department of Health Records and Statistics, Texas State Library. Indexes Microform: Texas Vital Statistics, 1956–1995.

Rosenberg Library, Galveston and Texas History Center, Galveston, Texas.

Galveston City Mortuary Books, 1875–1926.

Historical Mounts File.

Manuscript Collection:

MSS# 04-0028, J. Focke Papers; MSS# 05-0007, Red Cross Records; MSS# 22-0045, Anonymous Letter; MSS# 24-0149, Galveston Central Relief Committee Records; MSS# 28-0175+, T. L. Monagan Papers; MSS# 29-0028, Ben C. Stuart Papers, Box 1, Folder 39; MSS# 46-0006, J. D. Blagden Papers; MSS# 67-0042, J. H. Hawley Papers; MSS# 68-0009, M. Nicholson Papers; MSS# 73-0344, A. Block Papers; MSS# 76-0016, Minot Family Papers, Box 1, Folder 2; MSS# 79-0023, G. D. Scholes Papers.; MSS# 80-0019, Baltimore Committee in Aid of the Galveston Sufferers Souvenir Programme; MSS# 80-0021, L. R. Fayling Papers; MSS# 83-0017, I. S. Austin Papers; MSS# 83-0054, Louisa Christina Rollfing Papers; MSS# 85-0013, James Brown Papers; MSS# 85-0020, U.S. Commerce Department, Weather Bureau Records; MSS# 89-0016, Gonzales Family Papers, Box 2, Folder 15; MSS# 89-0018, Walker W. Davis 1900 Storm Letter; MSS# 91-0012, 1900 Storm Letter; MSS# 93-0023, William Maury Darst Papers, Box 2, Folder 3; Box 14, Folder 13; Box 42, Folder 15; MSS# 93-0026, 1900 Storm Letter; MSS# 95-0002, U.S. National Weather Service Records; MSS# 97-0020, Sarah Davis Hawley Papers, Box 1, Folder 14.

Map Collection: no. 456 B, Galveston Storm 1900.

Oral History Collection:

Beal, Emma; Bettencourt, Henry J.; Bettencourt, Margaret Rowan; Block, Hyman S.; Bristol, William M.; Goodman, R. Wilbur; Harris, John W.;

Hopkins, Louise; Nilson, Ellen Edwards; Pauls, Katherine Vedder.
Photograph Collection:
Name File.
Galveston Subjects File: 1900 Storm.
Special Collections and Photo Albums.

UNPUBLISHED SOURCES

Davis, Albert M., Jr., "Galveston's Bulwark against the Sea: History of the Galveston Seawall." Paper presented at the 2d Annual Conference on Coastal Engineering, Houston, Tex., November, 1951.

Harrowing, Frank Thomas. "The Galveston Storm of 1900." Master's thesis, University of Houston, 1950.

PUBLISHED SOURCES

Beasley, Ellen and Stephen Fox. *Galveston Architecture Guidebook.* Houston: Rice University Press, 1996.

Coulter, John, ed. *The Complete Story of the Galveston Horror.* New York: United Publishers of America, 1900.

Galveston, Texas, City Directory. Galveston: Morrison and Fourmy, 1880–1913.

Green, Nathan, ed. *Story of the Galveston Flood: Complete, Graphic, Authentic.* Baltimore: R. H. Woodward, 1900.

Griffin, S. C. *History of Galveston, Texas: Narrative and Biographical.* Galveston: A. H. Cawston, 1931.

Halstead, Murat. *Galveston: The Horrors of a Stricken City; Portraying by Pen and Picture the Awful Calamity that Befell the Queen City on the Gulf and the Terrible Scenes that Followed the Disaster.* Chicago: American Publishers' Association, 1900.

Henry, Walter K., Dennis M. Driscoll, and J. Patrick McCormack. *Hurricanes on the Texas Coast.* College Station: Texas A&M University Press, 1975.

Hodgkinson, Peter E., and Michael Stewart. *Coping with Catastrophe: A Handbook of Post-Disaster Psychosocial Aftercare.* 2d ed. London: Routledge, 1998.

Larson, Erik. *Isaac's Storm: A Man, a Time, and the Deadliest Hurricane in History.* New York: Crown, 1999.

Lester, Paul. *The Great Galveston Disaster, Containing a Full and Thrilling Account of the Most Appalling Calamity of Modern Times.* Promotional ed., abridged. Chicago: A. B. Kuhlman, 1900.

———. *The Great Galveston Disaster, Containing a Full and Thrilling Account of the Most Appalling Calamity of Modern Times.* Galveston: J. Singer, 1900.

McComb, David G. *Galveston: A History.* Austin: University of Texas Press, 1986.

McLeRoy, Sherrie. *Daughter of Fortune: The Bettie Brown Story.* Plano: Republic of Texas Press, 1997.

Malone, Dumas, ed. *Dictionary of American Biography.* Vol. 13. New York: Charles Scribner's Sons, 1934.

Malsch, Brownson. *Indianola: The Mother of Western Texas.* Austin: State House Press, 1988.

Mason, Herbert Molloy. *Death from the Sea: Our Greatest Natural Disaster, the Galveston Hurricane of 1900.* New York: Dial Press, 1972.

Miller, Ray. *Ray Miller's Galveston.* 2d ed. Houston: Gulf, 1993.

Newburn, Tim. *Disaster and After: Social Work in the Aftermath of Disaster.* London: Jessica Kingsley, 1993.

Ousley, Clarence, ed. *Galveston in Nineteen Hundred: The Authorized and Official Record of the Proud City of the Southwest as It Was before and after the Hurricane of September 8, and a Logical Forecast of Its Future.* Atlanta: William C. Chase, 1900.

Preston, Wheeler. *American Biographies.* 1st ed. New York: Harper and Brothers, 1940.

Raphael, Beverley. *When Disaster Strikes: How Individuals and Communities Cope with Catastrophe.* New York: Basic Books, 1986.

Scharnweber, William A., ed. *Facts about Galveston, Texas, the Deep Water Harbor of the Gulf of Mexico.* Galveston: A. A. Finck, 1899.

Schneider, Saundra K. *Flirting with Disaster: Public Management in Crisis Situations.* Armonk, N.Y.: M. E. Sharpe, 1995.

Simmen, Edward. *With Bold Strokes: Boyer Gonzales, 1864–1934.* College Station: Texas A&M University Press, 1997.

Tyler, Ron, ed. *New Handbook of Texas.* Austin: Texas State Historical Association, 1996.

United States Bureau of the Census. *Twelfth Census of the United States, Galveston County, Texas.* Vol. 44, 1900.

Weems, John Edward. *A Weekend in September.* New York: Holt, 1957.

Worley, John F. *John F. Worley & Co.'s Dallas Directory for 1900.* Dallas: John F. Worley, 1900.

INDEX

Pages containing illustrations appear in italics.

Adoue and Lobit Bank, 20
African Americans, 80, 85, 107–109, 110, 131, 133, 143–46, 183; armed, 87; looting, 116; shot, 40, 134
Alta Loma, Tex., 100, 128
Amundson, Gus, 81
Ashton Villa. *See* Brown residence
Austin, Henry, 67, 71
Austin, Ida Smith, 8, 9, 67–72
Austin, Tex., 66
Austin, Valery E., 67, 68
Austin residence, 68, *69*
Aziola Club, 39

Bader, Charles H., 153
Baldinger, Dr. William H., 78, 79, 80
Ball High School, 22, 129
Bardash, Hortense, 31
Barton, Clara, 75, 90–92, 160
Bath Avenue School, *52*
Beach Hotel, *97*
Beadles, Louise Hertford, 52, 55
Beadles, Walter "Bess," 52, 55
Beal, Crawford Montgomery, 149
Beal, Emily Peale Chappell, 149
Beal, Emma Bernie, 9, 149–51, *150*
Beers, Kenison and Company, 19
Bettencourt, Henrietta Oppenbrink, 151
Bettencourt, Henry, 151–52, *151*
Bettencourt, Margaret Rowan, 151, 152–55
Bishop's Palace. *See* Gresham residence
Black, Winifred, 8, 36–41
Blagden, John, 9, 15–19
Block, Alice, 49–52
Block, Fannie Kahn, 155
Block, Gertrude, 155
Block, Henry, 155
Block, Hyman, 155–61, *156*
Block, Leopold, 155, 158
Block, Mamie, 155
Block, Maurice, 49, 50–51
Block, Rosa (mother of Alice), 49, 50–51
Block, Rosa (sister to Hyman), 155, 160
Block, Sig, 49
bodies, 25–26, *27*, 34, 47, 54, 114, 136, 183; cremation, 26, 34, 37–38, 58, 70, 85, 99, 102–104, 114, 128, 135, 150, 160, 164, 172, 178; desecration, 34, 40, 137, 160, 178; morgue, 98–99, 160, *161;* taken to sea, 26, 34, *57*, 58, *59*, 70, 85, *99*, 103, 114, 128, 160, 164, 172, 178
Bornkessell, T. C., 14–15, 17, 19, 36, 42
Brashear, S. H., 91
bridges, 47, 63, 114, 124, *125*, 128, 136
Bristol, Cassandra Stump, 161–62, 170–73
Bristol, John William Stump, 162,
Bristol, Lois, 162,
Bristol, Mary Louise. *See* Hopkins, Mary Louise Bristol
Bristol, William H., 161, 170
Bristol, William Mason, 161–64

Broadway Memorial Presbyterian Church, 67, 71
Brokoff, Joe, 42–44
Brooks, Allen, 180
Brown, Bettie, 55, 63
Brown, James, 63–67
Brown, Sarah (Sallie), 63, 67
Brown residence, 62
Brush Electric Company, 69, *70*
Buffalo Bayou, 128

camps, military, 160, *162*, *163*. *See also* soldiers
Cannon, Fenelon, 150
Cavin, E. D., 62
churches: Broadway Memorial Presbyterian, 67, 71; First Baptist, 22; First Presbyterian, 67; Sacred Heart Catholic, *154*, 155; St. John's Methodist-Episcopal, 22; St. Mary's Cathedral, 156, 158; St. Patrick's Catholic, *71*
Citizens' Relief Committee, 39
Clamp, Winnifred Brown, 63, 66–67
Cline, Isaac M., 7, 13, 15–16, 19, 23, 36, 42, 49, 51, 156
Cline, Joseph L., 13, 15
Cohen, Rabbi Henry, 6
Committee of Public Safety, 56, 82–83
Conlon family, 22
Cornett, S. G., 61
Corrigan, Mr., 140–42
Cortes, Anna, 124
Cortes, Henry (the elder), 124
Cortes, Henry (the younger), 124–28

Daily, William, 31
Dallas Rough Riders, 93
Dallas, Tex., 5, 93
Dau, Frederick, 172
Davenport, Wharton, 58
Davis, Daisy, 33, 62
Davis, Emma, 28
Davis, Mary, 28
Davis, Walker W., 8, 45–49
Davis, Waters S., 28
Davis, Waters S., Jr., 33, 62
Davis, (Waters S.) residence, *29*, 29–30, 33
Denver Resurvey, 31, 63, 71, 175, 179, 184
Denver Resurvey School, 177
Dibrell, Charles, 140–41
Dibrell, Frances, 142, 145
Dibrell, James W., 139
Dibrell, Marsaline, 139, 142, 143, 144, 145, 146
Dickinson, Tex., 140–41

Edwards, Charity, 174
Edwards, Eliza, 174, 178
Edwards, James (brother of Ellen Nilson), 174, 176–78
Edwards, James (father of Ellen Nilson), 174
Elfstrom, Dorothy Bettencourt, 152
epidemic, fear of, 34, 114, 115

Fayling, Maj. Lloyd R. D., 8, 75–93, *76*
First Baptist Church, 22
First Presbyterian Church, 67
Fisher, Lillie Harris, 58, 169
Fisher, Walter, 57
Flatonia, Tex., 65
Fort Crockett, 5, 181

Gaither, Gordon, 104–106
Gallagher, Nicholas A. (bishop of Galveston), 159
Galveston Artillery Club, *120*
Galveston City Commission, 4
Galveston City Hall, 22, 152
Galveston City Park, 160, *163*
Galveston Cotton Exchange Building, 29
Galveston Cotton Mills, 62
Galveston County Commissioners, 4
Galveston County Courthouse, 158, *159*
Galveston Daily News, 56, 94; building, 104
Galveston Orphans' Home, 104–105, *105*
Galveston Waterworks, 110, *111*
Galveston Wharf Company, 3
Gill and League Building, 78, *79*

Goedhart and Bates, 5
Goff, Edward, 149
Gonzales, Boyer, 52
Gonzales, Julian "Alcie," 52, *55*
Goodman, Burleigh, 164, 165
Goodman, Florence May, 164
Goodman, Henry B., 164, 166
Goodman, Lawrence, 164
Goodman, Maria Louise, 164
Goodman, R. Wilbur, 164–67
grade-raising, 5
Grandison, James, 144–46
Grand Opera House, 22
Gresham residence, 31

Halstead, Murat, 6–7
Harris family, 31
Harris, Florence, 168
Harris, Guy, 51
Harris, John Woods II, 168–69
Harris, John Woods III, 168–70
Harris, Minnie Hutchings, 168
Harris, Rebecca, 31, 58, 169
Harris residence, *169*
Hawley, Harry, 28, 33–36, 56, 58
Hawley, Harry, Jr., 28, *35*, 56, 58
Hawley, Joseph Henry, 9, 56–63, 82–83, 87
Hawley, Julia Raine, 56
Hawley, Robert Bradley, 56, 60
Hawley, Sarah Davis, 28–36, 56, 58, 106
Heard, Bryan, 128
Hearde, Ed, 80
Heideman, Mrs. W. H., 31
Hendley Building, 152
Hertford, Eleanor, 8, 52–55
Hodson, Alice Minot, 19, 22
Hodson, George, 19–23
Hodson, John, 20
Hodson, Rebecca, 19
Holland, Victor, 140, 141
Hoodoos, 34
Hopkins, Mary Louise Bristol, 7, 161, 170–73
Houston, Tex., 5, 34, 37, 45, 48, 72, 90–93, 98, 104–105, 115–17, 124, 128
Houston Post, 56
Houston Ship Channel, 5
Huntington, Colis P., 3
Hurricane Alicia. *See* storm, 1983 (Alicia)
Hurricane Carla. *See* storm, 1961 (Carla)
Hutchins House, 91

Indianola, Tex., 3–4

Jenkins, Kate, 20–21
Jessen, Diedrich, 115
Jessen, Mina, 115, 117
John Sealy Hospital, 7, 13, *14*
Johnson, Willie R., 61
Jones, Mayor Walter C., 6, 41, 83, 85, 87, 92–93
Juenger, Vincenz, 117

Kane, Dan, 158
Kellner, Charles, Sr., 31
Kenison, Alphonse, 20, 21
Ketchum, Edwin N., 41, 75, 81, 83, 87–89, 134, 137
Kirwin, Rev. James M., 6, 83, 85
Knights of Pythias, 45, 155
Kopperl, Isabella, 31
Kopperl residence, *32*
Kuhnel, Ernest E., 15, 51–52

Lake Charles, La., 115, 117
Larson, Erik, 7
Law, Charles W., 9, 23–27
League City, Tex., 140, 146
League Park, 140
Lester, Paul 6–7
Levy (E. S.) Building, *17*
Levy, Marion, 160
Little Town Park. *See* League Park
Lobit, Bertha, 53
Longineau, Mrs. Thomas, 182
Longineau, Thomas, 182
looters, 36, 81, 99, 137, 178; shot, 18, 40, 65, 99, 104, 134, 137, 164, 178
Lord, Richard, 31

MacAshen, Annie, 142
martial law, 18, 37, 41, 45, 65, 81–90, 93, 100, 104, 160, 164
Marwitz house, 20, *21*
Mason, Francesca, 181
Mason, Herbert Malloy, Jr., 6–7
Mason, Kearny (the elder), 182
Mason, Kearny (the younger), 181
Massey, Pat, 43
Masterson, Anna (Mrs. Branch T.), 63
Masterson family, 31
Maxson, Harry, 9, 129–39
Maxson, Isadora, 129–30
Maxson, Willis, 129, 131, 136–37
McCaleb, Col. Hunt, 135
McKibben, Gen. Chambers, 101
McMaster, Charles H., 100
McVitie, William A., 34, 58
Mensing Building, 160
Michaelis, Charles J., 124
Miller, Sylvan, 156, 158
Miller, William P., 176
Miller Brothers, 156, 160
Minor, Lucian, 63, 180
Monagan, Thomas L., 101–104
Mott, Marcus, 29
Munn, James W., 182
Murdoch's Bathhouse, 77, *175*

Nagel, Gustav, 42, 45
Nave, Dr. William, 78, 79, 80
Nicholson, Martin, 42–45
Nilson, Ellen Edwards, 174–79
Noble, Alfred, 4

Oak Lawn. *See* Austin residence
O'Keefe bathing pavilion, 76–77
Ousley, Clarence, 6, 9, 94

Paget, Capt. Ormond, 93
Pagoda bathhouse, 77, *77*
Pauls, Katherine Vedder, 179–85
Peacock, Fannie, 23
Peek, Richard Hope, 31, 71, 180, 183
Perkins, Liza, 178
Port Bolivar, Tex., 3

Quinn, Johnny, 176–77, 179
Quinn, Mary, 174–76, 178

railroads: boxcars, 141, *141*; passenger trains, 95, 124; track, laying of, 136, *138*
Rafferty, W. C., 83
relief work: clothing, 62, 65, 72, 173; financial assistance, 45, 62, 72, 90; stations, 39; trains, 37, 48, 101, 104
Rice, E. E., 62, 121, 122
Ripley, Claud Gary, 31
Ripley, Henry Clay, 4
Ritters Saloon, 31, *32*
Robert, Henry M., 4
Robinson, Jennie, 49
Robinson, Maggie, 20–21
Rogers, Capt. Ed, 82, 90
Rollfing, Atlanta, 106, 107, 114, 115
Rollfing, August, Jr., 106, 107, *108*, 109, 112, 114, 115, 117
Rollfing, August, Sr., 106–107, 109–12, 114, 115, 116, 118
Rollfing, Fred, 110, 111
Rollfing, Helen, 106, 107, 109, 115
Rollfing, Louisa Christina, 7, 9, 106–17
Rosenberg Library, 7, 13, 15
Rosenthal, A. R., 90
Rowan, Hunter, 152
Rowan, Julius, 152
Rowan, Kathleen "Kate" Wallstein, 152
Rowan, Louisa, 152
Rowan, Margaret Catherine. *See* Bettencourt, Margaret Rowan
Rowan, William J., 152
Rowan, William F., 152
Runge, Forrest, 134
Russell, Alexander, 166

Sacred Heart Catholic Church, *154*, 155
St. John's Methodist Episcopal Church, 22
St. Mary's Cathedral, 156, 158

St. Patrick's Catholic Church, *71*
Sampson, Dr. Arthur, 34
San Antonio, Tex., 5, 48
Santa Fe Railroad, 129, 136
Sayers, Gov. Joseph D., 6, 75
Schirmer, William, 43
Scholes, Charles D., 140
Scholes, Geneva Dibrell, 139–46
Scholes, Robert, 139, 140–42, 143, 144, 145, 146
Scholes, Robert Dibrell, 139, 145
schools: Ball High, 22, 129; Bath Avenue, *52;* Denver Resurvey, 177
Scurry, Brig. Gen. Thomas, 75, 85, *86,* 88, 89, 92, 93, 100
Sealy, John, 90
Sealy residence, 31
Sears, Gen. W. H., 91, 92
Seawall: bonds, 5; plans for construction, 4
Shaw family, 22
ships: *Lawrence,* 90; *Mexican,* 28, 34, 58
slate (and other flying debris), 29, 51, 78, 80, 119, 121, 131, 165, 173
soldiers, 37, *38,* 81–91, *100,* 101, 160, *163,* 181. *See also* camps, military
Southern Pacific Railroad, 3, 164
Spencer, Stanley G., 31, 62
Spillain, Richard, 34
Springer, Col., 90
Star Clothing House, 156, 158
Star Drug Store, 126
Sterrett, Col. William G., 101, 102, 104
storm, 1875, 3–4
storm, 1900; death toll, 4, 11, 31, 33, 38, 47, 57, 70, 97, 98, 99, 114, 123, 136; property loss estimates, 4, 13, 70, 98; published works, 6–7; storm tides, 12, 20, 29, 42–43, 46–47, 50, 64, 95, 127, 166, 168, 180–81; warnings, 11, 12, 20, 56, 64, 68, 75, 77–78, 94–95, 106, 118, 140, 156, 163, 180; wind velocity, 12, 29, 47, 68, 94, 131
storm, 1915, 5, 143
storm, 1961 (Carla), 5
storm, 1983 (Alicia), 6
streetcars, 46, *46,* 104, 129, 165
Stuart, Ben C., 6, 9, 94–100
Swain, Richard, 58

Texas City, Tex. 24, 37, 90, 92, 98, 101, 105, 115, 160
Texas Heroes Monument, 120
Thomas, W. D., 105
Thornton, Lee, 34
Tremont Hotel, 23, 24, *25,* 45, 46, 47, 81, 88, 92
Tuffly, Louis J., 92

U.S. Weather Bureau, 11–12, 14–16, *17,* 19, 23, 36, 42, 49, 51, 94, 118, 131, 163

Vedder, Charles A., 179–83
Vedder, Florence Shryver, 179, 182, 183, 184
Vedder, Jacob, 180, 183
Vedder, Margaret, 184
Viehman, Frederick, 113
Vieno, J. Edwin, 20
Virginia Point, Tex., 47, 101, 140–41

Wagstaff, Anna, 145
Wagstaff, Frank, 145
Wakelee, Harriet, 57
Wallstein, Dorothy "Dora," 155
Walker, Alma, 127
Walker, Frank, 127
Walthew, Frank, 62
water, drinking, 100, 128, 142–44, 159, 177
Weems, John Edward, 6–7, 124
Willis, Mary "Mamie" Hawley, 28, 34–35, *35,* 56
Wilson, Richard, 28, 33, 35
Wolfram, Arnold R., 8, 118–23
Woollam's Lake, 57
Wolston, Mrs. Clint, 157
Wolston, Clint, Jr., 157
Wright, Alec M., 140–41

YMCA building, 78, 164